PUT YOUR
DEBT
ON A
DIET

PUT YOUR
DEBT
ON A
DIET

A STEP-BY-STEP GUIDE
TO FINANCIAL FITNESS

STANLEY J. KERSHMAN, LL.B.

John Wiley & Sons Canada, Ltd.

National Library of Canada Cataloguing in Publication

Kershman, Stanley J.
    Put your debt on a diet : a step-by-step guide to financial fitness / Stanley J. Kershman.

Includes index.
ISBN 0-470-83349-1

    1. Debt. 2. Finance, Personal. I. Title.

HG179.K478 2003   332.024'02   C2003-905469-1

Production Credits
Cover & interior text design: Interrobang Graphic Design Inc.
Printer: Tri-Graphic Printing Ltd.
Printed in Canada
10 9 8 7 6 5 4 3 2 1

Contents

Acknowledgements

I consider myself extremely fortunate to have had a sound and early education in matters of finance, and it has been one of my life's goals to share my knowledge with others. This book is the achievement of that goal and I hope that you will gain wisdom and understanding from its pages.

This book is dedicated to the memory of several outstanding people who have inspired me, taught me, and encouraged me throughout my life. First, my father, Harry Kershman, of blessed memory. No one could want for a better, more loving and understanding father. It has been six long years since his passing and I still miss him dearly. He was a soft-spoken man who understood what life was all about and who lived by those principles.

Second, my grandparents, Kayla and William Bodovsky, of blessed memory. They helped raise my brother John and me, and taught us the morals and values of a generation who struggled, survived and thrived through the depression and two world wars.

Third, my uncle Harry Leikin, of blessed memory. He came to Canada as a watchmaker and turned to the land to become a farmer and cattle buyer. With insight and perseverance, he created a real estate empire that fulfilled his dream of going from rags to riches, but never forgot his roots. He would look out from his farm and see the city lights flickering in the distance and would say to his foreman, Gurdev Bal, "I hope the city continues to grow this way." And it did.

Fourth, Issie and Shirley Kardish, of blessed memory. This loving couple, in their own quiet way and always with a smile on their faces, made charitable causes a priority in their lives and in the lives of those at the Rideau Bakery.

And last, to a woman I never knew but wish I had, my wife Carol's late mother—Rose Mary Ayers, of blessed memory. It is to her and Alfred Ayers that I owe my thanks for raising such a wonderful daughter, whom I had the privilege to meet, marry, and have a family with.

I'd like to thank many others who have helped make this book possible, as well. First, I want to thank G-d for His generosity in providing me with all the many gifts and opportunities that He has given me over my lifetime.

Many thanks to Rabbi Reuven Bulka for his inspiration; and to Mark Buckshon, Michael Wollock, Arron Fishbain, David Murdoch, Bev Murdoch, John McKeown, Mazal Ly, and my mother, Sylvia Kershman, for reading the drafts of the chapters and providing their helpful suggestions for improvement. Special thanks to Elaine Kenney of Communication Matters, Dov Vinograd, Les Morin, Royce Perry, and Lesley LeMarquand.

Thank you very much to Robert Harris, Karen Milner, Elizabeth McCurdy, Jamie Broadhurst, Robert Hickey, Lucas Wilk, Meghan Brousseau, Kari Romaniuk, Kimberly Rossetti, and Parisa Michailidis at John Wiley & Sons Canada, Ltd. for their continuing dedication and support in the writing and publishing of this book.

A special thank you to Monique van Remortel for her guidance with the legal aspects of book contracts.

Extra bonus thanks to Linda Poitevin who worked closely with me to make the writing of this book a gratifying experience, and without whom it would never have seen the light of day. A special thank you to John Lawford for his assistance also.

To my legal assistant, Mary Neill, many thanks for her computer skills, internet research, and transformation of my steadily declining penmanship into a workable manuscript.

My gratitude to Stanley Devine, Issie Rose, Harvey Slipacoff, Robert Abelson, and the "boys" at Dunn's Famous Delicatessen on Elgin Street, Ottawa for their many stories. This is the best place in the world for a delicious Montreal-style smoked meat sandwich.

A special thank you to my mother Sylvia Kershman for her many years of love and mentoring, without which I would not be where I am today.

Thank you to my wife, Carol, and my children, Zev and Kayla, for the support and sacrifices they made while I was writing this book. My wife has been an angel throughout and I am extremely grateful. Carol has been a particularly good teacher to Zev and Kayla about money management, increasing their knowledge and prudent use of it. My greatest hope is that my children and others will be able to learn from this book and put these principles into practice.

Stanley J. Kershman

Problems are simply solutions in waiting.™

REQUEST TO YOU, THE READER

I have a request. If this book has changed your life, I want to hear about it. Let me know what you have done differently as a result of reading this book. Do you have any tips that I can pass on to future readers? Do you have a favourite story, quote or insight into budgeting and finances that you would like to share? Just write, fax or email me at the address below.

If you have any comments, opinions, or are interested in having me conduct seminars or workshops for your group or association, please contact me.

Stanley Kershman Books
c/o Perley-Robertson Hill & McDougall LLP
400-90 Sparks Street
Ottawa, Ontario
Canada
K1P 1E2
Email: skershman@perlaw.ca
Fax: (613) 238-8775

Introduction

- Canadians currently owe more than $458 billion in debt. That's almost $15,000 for every man, woman, and child in this country.

- More people in this country are in debt than ever before because of mortgages, vehicle loans, credit cards, student loans, and other choices.

- The number of consumer bankruptcies has been rising dramatically every year.

These figures *should* scare you. Right now, Canadians are spending themselves into oblivion. The debt load isn't just high any more, it's *dangerously* high. It affects people from all walks of life—from the working poor to the highest-income professionals. And it will just get worse if we don't take control *now*.

Life wasn't easy when I was growing up, but by today's standards, it was certainly much simpler. You worked hard, bought what you could afford, saved a little, and above all, avoided debt. For as long as I can remember, these were the lessons that my parents taught my brother and me by their own example.

We lived modestly, very modestly, in a one-bedroom apartment above my grandparents. My brother and I shared the bedroom, and my parents had a pullout couch in the living room. From the time I was eight, I worked at my parents' drycleaning business, cleaning out the dryer for the change that fell from clothing. I received an allowance, and was expected to be responsible for my own money.

Would I rather have been rich? With a child's envy, you bet I would have, especially as I watched most of my friends go home after school to their big, fancy houses on the better side of town. But even as I grew up, it never once crossed my mind to try to be rich on credit.

Today, however, it's a different story. *"You are always pre-approved, live richly,"* trumpets the bold statement on a Toronto billboard. If only it was that simple.

Marketers would certainly like us to believe it is. "Why wait when you can have it all now?" they urge us. "Buy now, pay later. No interest, no payments for a full year. Use your credit card and save 20 per cent right now. Don't pay a cent...."

These messages, and many more like them, couched in splashy, sophisticated advertisements, try very hard to convince us that we need a brand-new car, fancier electronics, new furniture, designer eyewear...and whatever else they'd like to sell us. Then, just to make sure we can afford all these things, they flood our mailboxes with pre-approved credit card forms, low-interest loan offers, and limited-time-only, one-of-a-kind deals.

But is the have-it-all, have-it-now hype really that simple? Can we really afford the lifestyle the marketers would like us to believe we should have? Can we all live richly?

For the huge majority of people, the answer is no (as you may have already discovered), because pre-approval and zero interest aside, all of these offers ultimately mean one thing, and one thing only: debt. A lot of debt.

We can't blame all of our financial woes on the credit card companies and advertising agencies, however, because we have to be willing to buy into their messages for them to succeed in the first place. And the blame for doing that, unfortunately, falls squarely on our own shoulders.

Too many of us take for granted the things that allow us to pre-qualify for "living richly" in the first place (job security, financial stability, credit rating). We use these pre-qualifications as our financial foundations, only to find out how unstable they really are when we overextend ourselves or fail to plan for the unexpected.

Only one truly solid foundation for financial success exists, in my opinion, and that is a combination of education and communication, both of which are sadly lacking in our society. Beyond the concept of compound interest, money management isn't taught in most schools, and for some reason we seem to have imposed a "money taboo" upon ourselves—a reluctance to discuss money in anything but the most general terms. We're happy to talk about the economy, or to discuss the sudden downturn in the markets, but ask someone how they manage their credit card debt or avoid the paycheque-to-paycheque pitfalls, and the conversation is abruptly over.

You might argue, of course, that personal finances are just that—personal. I agree...to a point. Unfortunately, this reluctance to discuss money, even with the people who are most important to us, can undermine the most well-intentioned financial plan because we just don't have the necessary solid foundation.

So with no real education about money or managing credit, a reluctance to talk about them, and the constant temptation to abuse them, where does it end?

Regrettably, and all too often, in an office much like my own. In my 25 years of insolvency experience, I have seen an alarming increase in the number of people running into financial difficulties.

- In 1976, just over 10,000 consumers filed for bankruptcy.

- In 1986, consumer bankruptcies rose to 21,765.

- In 1991, that number tripled to 62,277.

- In 2002, the number increased again, to more than 78,000.

- In 2003, consumer bankruptcies are expected to reach 82,000.

It is painfully obvious to me that the way we handle our finances just isn't working. Canadians are currently about two paycheques away from bankruptcy. Our salaries simply cannot keep pace any longer with our ever-increasing spending. It's time to face reality and to stop buying into the marketers' falsehoods.

To me, the whole "live rich on credit" philosophy makes about as much sense as an "eat all you want of whatever you want and still lose weight" kind of diet. You can't *have it all* and expect healthy finances any more than you can *eat it all* and expect a healthy body. It just doesn't work that way.

We cannot continue to rely on credit to achieve the rich lifestyle that marketers want us to believe we're entitled to. Even if we manage to keep up appearances for a while, at the first sign of financial stress (job loss, illness, unexpected expenses) our foundations can begin to crumble, toppling us into financial disaster.

That's not to say that you can't live richly, however, if that's what's important to you. You may never be a multi-millionaire (or fit into your high school jeans again!), but you may very well be able to have that big-screen TV, or take that Caribbean cruise, or even buy that waterfront property. You just can't do it all right now, no matter what the ads (or the diets) say.

Instead, you need to take the time to build truly healthy finances that will provide you with the stability you need to move forward. This means reducing your debt, educating yourself and your family, and making sure your foundation is solid.

Have dreams and goals, but achieve them on your own terms, not the marketers'. And realize that more money isn't the answer; smarter management of the money you already have *is*.

CHAPTER ONE

Weighing In

Assessing Your Financial Picture

*"Too many people spend money they haven't earned, to buy things
they don't want, to impress people they don't like."*
—Will Rogers

Getting into debt can happen to anyone—it's not how much money
you have, it's what you do with it.

Poor financial habits can have the same devastating effect on
your life as poor eating habits. Put on a few extra pounds here and
a few more there, start skipping meals or neglecting basic nutrition
and exercise, and your health and energy suffer.

It's the same with your finances. Run up a credit card here, an
RRSP loan there, neglect to save for the unexpected or to keep track
of your cheque book...you see my point.

Unfortunately, there's no such thing as a "miracle *debt* pill" any
more than there is a "miracle *diet* pill" (no matter how much we'd
like to believe in one!). There are no quick fixes for overstrained
budgets and finances, no magic wands that will zap away maxed-out
credit cards, no overnight cures that will suddenly reverse the flow
of money in your life.

If and when you decided to lose weight or get in shape, you
wouldn't (or at least shouldn't) dive headlong into an unsupervised,
unhealthy fad diet, or begin training at an Olympic-athlete level.
The proven path to success would mean evaluating your health now,
setting goals, and planning a realistic path to reach those goals.

Exactly the same principles hold true for your finances.

Reducing your debt and taking control of your financial future, like making any other lasting lifestyle change, will take both effort and time. You're going to have to examine everything from your cheque book to your life priorities, and you'll to have to rethink just about everything you ever knew, or thought you knew, about money. And to succeed, you'll need to do all of this in a sensible, well-planned way.

FACING THE SCALE

To make sure that you choose the right plan of action for your financial situation, you need to know where you are now. Take off the rose-coloured glasses and have an honest look in the mirror—and at your situation. You may not like what you see, but at least you'll know the truth about where you're starting.

Be sure you look at your entire financial picture, not just the parts you're comfortable with. This includes your current debt load, your assets, and your objectives. Think of it as a physical exam for your finances!

Monthly income/expenses can fluctuate widely, depending on seasonal or quarterly expenses like insurance, water bills, or heating costs, and on whether you're working on commission or in a seasonal industry like tourism. You'll get a better idea of your true financial picture by looking at your expenses over an entire year—and before you panic, this is a lot easier than it sounds.

Start by weighing your current net income against your spending output. This is as simple as taking a sheet of paper and dividing it into two columns. On one side, write down the money you have coming in. Include your net paycheque, any investment income, pension income, and things like child tax credits (family allowance). Multiply these out to get a yearly amount (for instance, if your paycheque is bi-weekly, you would multiply your net income per cheque by 26 pay periods). The exercise becomes more challenging if you are working in a seasonal industry, but it still works (remember that there may be a combination of paycheque income and employment insurance benefits in this situation).

Then, tackle the other side of the paper. You'll have to do some homework for this part by gathering information about your household expenses, including house and car payments, utilities, clothing and entertainment expenses, groceries, transportation, insurance (life, house, and vehicle), club or school fees, magazine subscriptions...everything you can think of. Write down each of these expenses, and once you think you have them all, take out your credit card statements for the past six months to see if you've missed anything.

Again, turn your expenses into annual figures. You can now create an Income and Expense Statement, an example of which is included in Appendix "A". Now take a deep breath and compare your annual income to your expenses. You may be shocked by what you see, but don't be discouraged. This is only the first step, and reality can be a sobering experience for anyone.

If your income outweighs your expenses by a significant amount, but you're still struggling with a heavy debt load and can't say where all the extra goes—keep reading.

If you're just meeting your expenses with little or nothing left over, you could be only a few short steps away from trouble—keep reading.

If what you're spending outweighs what you're earning, you're already *in* trouble, and you need to take immediate and drastic action to avoid serious financial problems—keep reading!

In addition, you will also need to make an inventory of your assets and liabilities in order to determine your net worth. An example of a Net Worth Statement has been included in Appendix "B".

DANGER SIGNALS:

How to Recognize if You're Facing (Serious) Financial Trouble

• You're out of money before your next paycheque.

- You're late paying bills.

- You're relying on cash advances from credit cards to get you through to the next paycheque.

- You're receiving demand letters and/or phone calls from your creditors or collection agencies.

- Your creditors are suing you.

- Your salary or bank account has been garnisheed.

- Your credit rating has been downgraded.

EXAMINING YOUR MONEY ATTITUDES

When you sit down with your spouse or partner to discuss financial goals, chances are you'll discover that he or she has an entirely different approach to money than you have. One of you may prefer to pay cash for everything, the other may see no problem with using credit. These traits can often be traced back to our parents' attitudes about money. Most people will mimic what they grew up with ("if it was good enough for Mom and Dad, it's good enough for me"), or in some cases, rebel against it ("I never had anything I wanted when I was growing up and I won't do the same thing to my own kids").

Also, many people grow up in families that don't discuss money (at least, not reasonably—having your father or mother yell about how the family can't afford those things isn't quite the discussion I have in mind). Consequently, they never learn the importance, or the benefits, of talking openly about money matters and having their families understand the workings of everyday finances.

If you haven't been communicating openly about money until now, the differences in how you manage your finances have probably been causing considerable tension in your family. Before you forge ahead with a new financial strategy, or begin trying to negotiate compromises, it helps to accept, or at least understand, the reasons for these differences.

Generally speaking, the population can be divided into two groups: spenders and savers. Spenders tend to favour instant gratification. They're the ones most likely to buy into the have-it-all, have-it-now ideology; they feel the need to spend any money that they have, and often any money (in the form of credit) that they don't have.

Savers, on the other hand, favour delayed gratification. They are constantly tucking away their money into investment funds—an RRSP account here, a mutual fund there, a vacation fund somewhere else.

While conflict is most likely to happen when a spender and saver get together (they probably won't agree on anything to do with money at first!), problems can also arise from a spender/spender or a saver/saver combination.

Spender/spender couples buy into the easy-credit hype and can very quickly run themselves into financial difficulty. They need to be very honest about their spending habits and have a clear, written plan of action that they both agree to follow.

Even saver/saver couples can run into difficulty when they have different ideas about *how much* and *how to*. A hyper-saver may complain that a saver isn't saving enough, and secretly feel that the saver is really a spender in disguise.

Whatever the couple combination, and whatever the financial problems being faced, open communication remains the key to successful resolutions.

Set a specific time to discuss your finances with your partner. A good time might be after dinner, once the kids are in bed and the dishes are dealt with. (A bad time would be when you're in the middle of balancing the cheque book or paying the overdue bills.)

If you think that present conflicts might erupt into an all-out war, take the conversation to neutral territory. You're less likely to get involved in a yelling match if you're sitting in a coffee shop instead of your living room.

Share your history with your partner. How did your family handle their finances/budget discussions? Has it affected you? How? Ask your partner about the money messages he/she grew up with.

Take turns telling each other what worries you about your partner's spending/saving habits. Don't be afraid to say what you admire, too. Spenders are often in awe of the way savers can set limits and live within them, and savers may secretly like a partner's ability to enjoy the moment. People think that if they express any kind of appreciation for their partner's traits, it gives them permission to continue the behaviour, but it's often the positive statements that help us feel secure enough to let go of the negative behaviours or at least to compromise.

Once you've opened the door to communication and have a better understanding of where your partner is coming from history-wise, it's time to move ahead.

SETTING YOUR GOALS

Every successful diet begins with goals, and a debt diet is no different. In addition to knowing where you are now, you need to have a clear idea of where you want to be.

If you're reading this book, you've already decided to make reducing your debt load one of your goals, but what else is important to you? In general terms, do you want to simply be debt free? Do you want to be wealthy? Somewhere in between?

Think of specifics, too. Do you want to reduce your income tax? Set aside money for your children's education? Buy a new home or new car?

Don't forget to include your partner and children in decisions you make about your family's goals. Any changes you make to the way you handle your finances will affect not only your spending habits, but your family's as well. Let's face it, if you suddenly start serving vegetarian meals to your hamburger-loving kids without consultation, they're going to cry foul. And if you suddenly announce that your previously open-wallet policy is now closed until further notice, they'll yell even louder!

Your best chance of succeeding at improving your financial situation is with your family's cooperation and support. So get their feedback about your own suggestions, and ask for their ideas, too. Find out what's important to each of them, and what they're willing to compromise on. Share what's important to you. Not everyone's goals will be the same, so expect some initial conflict and be prepared to talk things through until you can all agree on some common ground.

Set up a journal for tracking your budget and family goals. Seeing things in black and white can have a greater impact than abstract-sounding numbers tossed around in conversation, and physically tracking your family's progress toward its goals can be a great motivator.

Be patient. You're introducing a lot of new concepts here, and it will take time for everyone to adjust. Think of it as learning to row a boat: At first everyone will be out of sync and it will feel like the boat is going nowhere, and perhaps even floundering. But once everyone is pulling together, your boat will glide effortlessly over the water.

And remember, too, that if you invite your family into the discussion, the bonus is that they'll be learning some valuable financial lessons along the way.

Break your goals down into short- and long-term ones. Think about where you want to be in a month, six months, a year, five years, or even a lifetime. Keep in mind that your objectives don't have to be complicated. Set small goals as well as larger ones, and be realistic.

SUCCESS TIP

Write down your objectives. Staying focused is easier with a visible target.

If you're a single-income family with three small children and you're barely making ends meet right now, don't expect to whisk the family off to Disney World next summer (even if that's *their* primary goal). Instead, decide that you want to feel more in control of your financial habits: Maybe this month's goal could be to gather all the information you need to get started. Or, if you're in a financial crisis, you could set up an appointment with a credit counsellor to review your situation (see Chapter Two). Nothing reaffirms your determination to succeed like success itself. And you will succeed!

CHAPTER SUMMARY

- Face the scale: Evaluate your current situation.
- Recognize credit-overuse danger signs.
- Examine your family's money attitudes.
- Set your goals and write them down.

Taking Control

Changing How You Manage Your Finances

"Advertising may be described as the science of arresting the human intelligence long enough to get money from it."
—Stephen Leacock, *Garden of Folly*

We all have basic *needs* in common: food, clothing, shelter, and transportation. Depending on our individual priorities, we also have an unlimited number of *wants*: vacations, trendy clothing, state-of-the-art electronics, new vehicles, and much, much more. The problem we face today is shrewd marketers whose job it is to convince us that many of our *wants* are actually *needs*—something that, judging by today's economy, they've become very adept at doing.

To gain control over your finances (just as you would your eating habits), you also need to gain control over your own impulses. You need to be able to clearly identify what is actually a *need* in your life (healthy, nutritious food, etc.), and where your *wants* (fast food, ice cream, alcohol, etc.) are crossing the line, and you need to help your family do the same. To begin making these distinctions, you have to learn to recognize the way that the media and marketers are influencing your priorities.

Take a pair of eyeglasses, for example. If you are prescribed corrective eyewear, glasses obviously become a need. But then the question of frames arises, and that's where the advertisers step in. There are many attractive frames available at a reasonable cost that would be perfectly suitable. Buy into the marketers' idea of suitable, however, and all of a sudden you *"need"* to have designer frames, complete with designer cost. Because of the money taboo that says you can't openly discuss your personal finances, you may also feel pressure (real or imagined) not to simply say that you can't afford the fancy frames. You may rationalize it another way and say that over five years it's only $5 a month. A mere pittance.

To further add to the marketing scheme, let's toss in that new credit card you're carrying, courtesy of the pre-approved credit card application that arrived in last month's mail. You remember, the one with the 8.9 per cent introductory interest rate that you filled out and returned so you'd have it just in case...and now you have everything you need to begin your downward financial slide: motive, means, and opportunity.

Warning!

A financial downslide involves:

- Motive (usually a want)
- Means (available credit)
- Opportunity ("reason" to buy)

Don't do it!

See how neatly the marketers cornered you? Your basic need got blown up into a muddled, seemingly attainable need/want, and you fell for it. Instead of paying cash for the affordable, attractive $100 frames, you now have a $350 charge on a new credit card (a card that you didn't need) so that you can sport a designer label (that you also didn't need) on your face.

But hey, $350 isn't really all that bad, is it? Make the minimum monthly payment on the card for a few months (so low that you'll hardly even feel a pinch), and you'll own your designer frames outright. Big deal!

Well, aside from the fact that you'll end up paying about $21 in interest over eight months at 8.9 per cent (bringing the cost of your fancy frames to a grand total of $371), let's run a little further with this particular ball. Let's say that the week after you purchase the glasses, your television bites the dust.

You've been expecting it to go, so maybe you've been putting a little bit aside every paycheque or so. You figure you can comfortably afford about $500—a decent 25-inch colour television. But when you get to the store, you're overwhelmed by the choices, the sales pitch, and maybe even by the number of people walking out the door with bigger, better televisions than what you came in for. Suddenly you remember that you've been thinking of upgrading your television system for years. After all, there's so much more available now.

Take that 42-inch, plasma-screen baby sitting front and center, for instance. The picture looks 3D and the sound is amazing. Wouldn't that look fabulous in the family room? And hey, it's on sale...and you have that nifty new credit card that you brought along *just in case*.

Reality Check

Ever stopped to consider the real cost of a credit card?

If you have a $3,000 balance on your card at 19.8 per cent interest, and make minimum payments of two per cent of the balance (or $15, whichever is greater), without making any new purchases, it will take almost 40 years to pay off the debt and cost more than $10,000 in interest charges.

Five thousand dollars plus tax later, and you're now making minimum payments on a credit card balance of $6,100 (including the glasses). Not quite as easy to justify...and now there's a definite pinch that's going to last for a much longer time.

So what's a person to do?

First, clearly identify your wants versus your needs. Recognize the daily media bombardment for what it is—a continuous series of marketing ploys. Be aware. Be skeptical. Involve your partner and family in purchase decisions and let cooler heads prevail. Educate your children about marketing practices (ever notice that on TV marketing ads for kids, they never mention the cost?) and talk openly about the need to be realistic.

And above all, get past any perceived shame in saying "we can't afford it." People need to hear this (and say it) loud and clear, and often. We were never meant to afford everything that marketers *want* us to have, and the reality is that we don't *need* everything. Don't become like a certain family in Montreal who told everyone that they went to Florida every winter, but in reality camped out for two weeks in their basement with supplies that included a sun lamp so that they could emerge with "Florida" tans!

Also, be aware of the "bargain" trap that tempts us all. Deals that sometimes seem too good to pass up can end up costing us far more than we initially bargained for. If you're tempted by such a deal (and aren't we all?), think carefully, apply the same need versus want questions, and once again let cooler heads prevail.

Just recently my friend Herb offered to sell me a very expensive home theatre system for $3,000. It included everything—a 52-inch screen TV, receiver, DVD player, cassette deck, remote control, and 10 speakers to put up throughout our home. Tempted? You bet. But my wife and I looked at it, thought about it, and asked ourselves these questions:

• Did we need it, or just want it?

• What other costs would be involved?

• What would it do to our lifestyle? Would we watch more TV? Did we want to? Did we want our kids to?

The answers we arrived at were sobering:

• It was definitely a want.

• As far as costs were concerned, I estimated that, to buy the system and have it moved and installed, it would cost about $5,000 to

$6,000. Plus we'd have a cable bill *increase* (for digital cable) of about $40 per month ($480 per year). Did we really need that additional expense? Definitely not.

• Our lifestyle would almost certainly change with the appeal of a big-screen television. We would all be inclined to watch more TV, and no, that was not something we wanted our kids to do.

Our conclusion, then, was that this "bargain" would be more than we had bargained for, both in actual costs and in the cost to our family relationship. Plus, we'd also be sending a message to our kids regarding wants that I wasn't sure I wanted to give them. Sorry, Herb...thanks, but no thanks!

While we didn't end up getting the system, I found it unsettling that I (who, in writing this book, should definitely know better) could be so tempted by impulse. But the truth is that you'll probably always be faced with these temptations, and it's in how you decide to handle them that you'll determine your own success or failure in changing your financial fortunes.

Beyond conquering your own wants, remember to help your kids identify theirs, as well. You've (hopefully) taught them what nutritious eating is, and talked about the health dangers of indiscriminately indulging their appetites for junk food. This is much the same. Teach them the difference between a right to which they're entitled, and a privilege that they must earn. If you let media and societal pressures (or junk food appetites) win over common sense, you're only helping to perpetuate the have-it-all-now myth (instant gratification)—not the kind of legacy you want to leave your kids.

RETHINKING YOUR DEBT TOLERANCE

People who don't monitor their diet and exercise habits often fail to see (or don't want to see) the potential darker side of their lifestyle choices: heart disease, diabetes, and a host of other ailments. The have-it-all-now myth has the same darker side to it (over and above simple consumer gullibility): the capacity to bring financial ruin through sheer short-sightedness.

Debt tolerance is a term used to describe the level of debt with which people are comfortable. This tolerance level will often change as people get older and become less willing to take risks with their finances or their futures.

Some people (like strict health-food advocates) are completely intolerant of debt to begin with, and will refuse to purchase anything unless they either have cash in hand or the ability to pay off their debt in full within 30 days.

At the other end of the scale are the overeaters, people who think it's safe to take on any number of debts as long as they can meet the minimum monthly payments. If you're among those who are comfortable with this kind of debt tolerance, it's time to think again—and read on!

THE CREDIT CARD TRAP:

10 Easy Steps to Getting Caught

1. You charge a few items a month, but pay off your balance in full. It's easy, convenient, and great for the bigger items when you don't have the cash.

2. Your balance grows beyond what you can pay off each month and you begin making the minimum payments.

3. You notice that a big chunk of your payment goes to interest charges; the outstanding balance continues to grow.

4. An emergency comes up. With no cash on hand, you charge it, promising that you'll pay it off when the bill comes.

5. The outstanding balance is so big that it takes all of your disposable income just to make the minimum payment.

6. Another emergency—and another charge.

7. You reach your limit and panic, but then...saved! Another pre-approved credit card application arrives in the mail. You take up the offer and get a new card.

8. Your monthly disposable cash gets tighter and tighter because of your payments. You need cash for an out-of-town business trip, so you take a cash advance...another charge.

9. Interest eats up more and more of your monthly payments, and the outstanding balance keeps growing...fast!

10. You've managed to max out all your cards. But how? You don't even remember what you bought! Your disposable income is no longer enough to pay the minimums. Late charges start adding up. Late notices begin to arrive....

TRAPPED!

The unfortunate reality of the minimum-monthly-payment mentality is that eventually you'll have so many debts that you'll run out of money to meet all of the minimum monthly payments, not to mention what would happen if you faced the loss of a job, a family illness, or some other potential disaster that could halt all or part of your family's income, even temporarily. At this point, there are several different paths you might take, all involving some kind of juggling act, and all leading to the same ultimate financial disaster.

If you decide to stop making one or two of the payments in order to meet your other obligations, or if you can't afford to make one or two payments, it's only a matter of time before creditors will begin calling to find out where their payments are and when you will be making them. Then you'll have to stop paying someone else in order to catch up on the already missed payments. The result: a juggling act of deciding which payments to make this month, and which to skip; and only a matter of time before all the balls you're trying to keep aloft tumble down around your head.

Or maybe you're a more sophisticated debtor. You can not only afford to make the minimum monthly payments, but if something unexpected does come up, you have enough available credit to withdraw what you need to cover your shortfall. If you're lucky, you have enough room on two or three credit cards so that you can continue to borrow whenever you need to, and keep your minimum monthly payments in good standing. Another juggling act—this one working until you've run out of available credit and your juggling balls once again tumble in disarray. Depending on the amount available, you could stay afloat for another six to 12 months. Once that is used up, however, the overwhelming weight of your debt will cause you to sink...fast.

No matter how well you think you're currently handling your debt load, you owe it to yourself and your family to take a long, hard, and honest look at your tolerance for debt and the resulting balance of your scale. If you've chosen the minimum monthly payment route, you're paying out phenomenal amounts of interest at best, and at worst taking a very dangerous path. The moment you become involved in any kind of juggling act, your finances are at serious risk and you need to completely—and immediately—rethink your approach.

TAKE ADVANTAGE OF AVAILABLE SERVICES

There is an unfortunate stigma attached to the idea of getting credit counselling. Too many people who wouldn't hesitate to seek help for virtually any other problem in their lives (including dieting) find shame in asking for help when it comes to handling their debt load and budget. The truth is that anyone who needs a credit counselling service can, and should, use it without hesitation...including doctors, lawyers, business professionals, and yes, even you.

SHOULD YOU SEEK CREDIT COUNSELLING?

If you answer "yes" to one or more of these questions, credit counselling can help:

- Do you ever use one credit card in order to pay another?

- Are you making only the minimum monthly payments on your credit cards or loans?

- Is more than 20 per cent of your monthly take-home pay being used for credit card and loan payments?

- Have you made late payments on any of your bills in the last three months?

- Are your creditors sending you past-due notices because of late payments?

- Have you been thinking of borrowing to consolidate your debts?

- Do you find it hard to prepare or stick with a budget?

- Are financial worries interfering with your sleep or your family life?

If you have the feeling that you're in over your head debt-wise, or you'd like some advice on how to deal with your specific financial situation, think about getting some help. Credit counselling agencies are located throughout Canada, and are usually non-profit organizations (a list of agencies is set out in Appendix "C").

Credit counselling agencies generally provide free, confidential credit and debt counselling (depending on your particular financial situation, you may be asked to make a small contribution towards ongoing counselling services), debt management programs, and personal budgeting sessions. Anyone can use their services regardless of age, sex, race, or income level. At the very least, credit counselling agencies have excellent materials available (both online and hard copy) to walk you through everything from setting up a budget to talking to your partner about your financial goals.

If you need more help than just reading materials, don't hesitate to ask for it. Counsellors are not there to judge you any more than a dietician will judge your eating habits when you ask for help. Their goal, and their job, is to help you learn how to handle your money and either reduce or eliminate your debt. To do this, they will work with you to create a budget specific to your circumstances, and suggest ways to trim expenses and increase income.

If necessary, counsellors can also speak with your creditors and ask them for their patience and understanding while you get through a financial crunch. They can set up an orderly payment of debts program, where you make a single monthly payment to the credit counselling agency, which in turn pays your creditors the agreed-upon amounts. One monthly payment for you, satisfied creditors, no more unwanted phone calls or letters—just imagine how much better you'll sleep, and how much less stress you and your family will have!

INDEPENDENT DEBT MANAGEMENT

If you want to put your debt on a diet and think you can do so without the assistance of a credit counsellor, here are some tips that will help.

Assuming that you're not yet at a crisis point in your debt (you haven't maxed out every card in your possession, and you're still meeting your payments on time, with some disposable income left over), but that you feel overextended:

• Immediately stop using your credit cards. Take them out of your wallet or purse, and put them somewhere not easily accessible (some people freeze them in a block of ice...also known as "putting your credit cards on ice"). By the time your cards thaw out, you've had the chance to rethink whatever need you thought you had. If you're really serious, cut them in half and toss them out (it's a good idea to keep one, but only one, for true emergencies).

- Pay off your outstanding balances. Do this *before* you begin your savings program. You'll save more by paying $100 on your 18.9 per cent interest card than you will by putting that same $100 into an eight per cent investment account.

Reality Check

If you made one extra payment a year of $100 on a 18.9% interest credit card, you would save at least $18.90 in interest payments—if you took that same $100 and invested it at 8% you would earn $8 in interest in the first year. If you kept it invested, it would take you over 11 years at 8% interest compounded annually to earn as much as you could have saved by paying that $100 on your credit card.

- If you're approaching a debt crisis (your payments are still on time, but you've pretty much maxed out all your cards and your payments now take up all of your disposable income): think about getting a consolidation loan (more about these in Chapter Four). Many banks and financial institutions offer these loans to help people get back on track towards financial health. Under a debt consolidation loan, your lender pays off all your other creditors and combines the debts into one loan, with one payment. Your financial "waistband" will immediately feel more comfortable, and you can start breathing again and concentrate on getting back on track.

CAUTION: If you consolidate your debts, you MUST close your lines of credit and credit cards in writing so that you're not tempted to use them again. Even after you've paid off your consolidation loan, don't fall back into the same credit trap that got you here in the first place. Now is the time to develop new habits (like paying cash) and to move forward, not backward, in your new-found financial health.

And most important of all: If you haven't started to accumulate any debt, don't!

- Be firm with yourself. Credit cards are only for emergencies, not for impulse buys!

- If you're just starting out and trying to build (or rebuild) a credit rating, there's a right way and a wrong way to do so. Hint: Running up massive amounts of debt on your credit cards would be the wrong way. (For more about credit ratings and histories, see Chapter Four.)

SUCCESS TIP

Before you whip out that credit card for your next purchase, remember your long-term goals and strategies:

- Does this purchase move you towards your goals?

- Does it fit with your strategies?

If the answer is no, leave your credit card where it is and walk away—stronger, financially healthier, and guilt free.

Effectively managing your debt is one of the first—and most important—steps toward your future financial health. Debt creates a constant drain on your finances, your peace of mind, and your personal relationships. It takes the money you need to build your family's financial future (emergency fund, retirement savings, kids' education) and puts it in the pockets of your creditors instead.

DEALING WITH ADDICTIONS

But what if the problem isn't yours? What if someone else in your family is playing havoc with the finances and you're doing everything you can just to keep the family afloat? It's as if your best efforts at sticking to your diet were being constantly undermined by someone force-feeding you all the wrong possible things.

Families who live with addictions can face devastating financial problems that can require making equally devastating decisions. Alcohol, drugs, gambling, and excessive shopping can all have serious repercussions when it comes to family budgets, and dealing with the results can seem overwhelming.

When Al and his wife, Jean, borrowed some money from me, I took a mortgage on their house. He and his wife had been bankrupt once and I wanted to help them out. They made the payments faithfully for about two years and then just stopped. I followed up with them and found out that they were once again in financial difficulty. Al finally admitted that it was due to his gambling. One month the payment came back NSF and I wrote Al a letter. He called and told me that he'd had the money, but had gone to a casino to "make more money." Guess what? Exactly. He'd lost the mortgage payment at the casino and didn't have any more money to make the payment.

I've given Al one final chance: I've told him that if he doesn't keep up the payments, he'll have to move out in 60 days. I've also urged him to get professional help for his addiction and he has said that he will. I hope he does, because otherwise I will have no choice but to repossess his home and sell it, as any other creditor would do under the same circumstances.

Addicts will go to great lengths to finance their addictions, even as they deny having them. I've seen people like Al go to the casino, take multiple cash advances of $500 or more from their credit cards (the largest cash advance you usually can get is $500 at a time, otherwise they'd almost certainly take more), and gamble away every cent. Imagine the shock when their partner (probably the secondary cardholder) opens up that month's credit card statement.

Of course, if the addict is particularly cunning, he or she will watch the mailbox and hide or destroy the statement when it does arrive. It could be months before their partner even knows about the problem.

Addicts need help, but so do their families and partners. If you suspect that you're living with an addict (financial signs might include cleaning out bank accounts; maxing out credit, including credit cards, credit lines, loans, and any overdraft protection; or selling valuables that may or may not belong to them), you need to protect yourself legally and financially. Leaving your finances in the hands of an addict will lead to financial and emotional disaster for you and your family. An addiction isn't some irritating habit that will eventually disappear or sort itself out. It's a serious problem that can result in major financial consequences, and it requires your immediate attention.

Cover Your Assets!

If you have to cancel a credit card:

- DO IT IN WRITING. Even if the card company tells you that a phone call is enough, it's not!

- Send your notification by registered mail.

- Request a written response and follow up to make sure that you get one.

- Keep copies of all correspondence for your records.

Even if you confront the addict and he or she agrees to seek help, take steps to ensure that your financial situation doesn't get any worse. Cut off access to your funds. If you have a joint account, close it (if the account is in overdraft, you'll have to pay it out first) and open another in your name only. Do the same with credit cards: Cancel the cards in writing via registered mail, and request a written acknowledgment from the credit card company. You'll be liable for any debt on the card up until the notification date, but at least it won't go any further. Some people think that if they don't use the card, or if they destroy it, they're not liable for the charges on it. Wrong. Regardless of who uses the card, if your name is on the account, you are liable.

In extreme cases, where you can prove an addiction, you may need to go to court to have the addict declared incapable of handling his or her own finances, and to have a power of attorney appointed to take over the addict's affairs. As draconian as this may sound, you could actually be helping the addict protect himself or herself by making it harder to feed the addiction and forcing him or her to get help.

Don't overlook the benefits of counselling for yourself and your family. Even if an addict will not get help, family members can and should do so in order to understand and learn how to cope with living with an addict.

Services that help addicts often help their families as well, or can point you in the direction of someone else who can. These include:

• Gamblers Anonymous (www.gamblersanonymous.org)

• Alcoholics Anonymous (www.alcoholics-anonymous.org)

• Debtors Anonymous (www.debtorsanonymous.org)

• Narcotics Anonymous (www.narcoticsanonymous.org)

CHAPTER SUMMARY

- Recognize the difference between *wants* and *needs*.

- Rethink your debt tolerance.

- Find out if you need credit counselling, and know where to find it.

- Independent debt management: Use the many tips for getting yourself on track.

- Act if addictions are straining family finances.

CHAPTER THREE

Your Budget

Five Steps to a More Beautiful Bottom Line

"I have not failed. I've just found 10,000 ways that won't work."
—Thomas Edison

In order to put your debt on a diet that will work, you need to do more than just discuss it with your family and set goals. You also need to have a written eating plan, or in financial terms, a budget.

You're probably cringing at the very word, but before you throw up your arms in despair and abandon the whole idea of ever gaining control over your debt and finances, hear me out.

The simple fact is that everything we've discussed so far—communication, goal-setting, breaking free of the have-it-all-now mentality, even credit counselling—*everything* has been leading up to this. Your family's entire financial future hinges on this one crucial step. Take the step—make the effort—and everything else will fall into place. Avoid it or decide it's not worth the trouble, and you'll be cheating yourself out of the full benefit of the other ideas in this book.

For any diet to be successful, and for you to be able to monitor your successes so that you know what's working and what isn't, some kind of tracking system is needed. As anyone who's ever dieted will tell you, writing things down keeps you honest...especially with yourself. Without such a tracking system, an extra few bites here and there can add up fast, and sabotage your entire diet.

The same holds true for a financial plan. An unplanned expenditure here and there and you're back to dreading your credit card statements and avoiding phone calls.

Your budget, then, is two things:

- A financial tracking system—the one tool that will truly put you in touch with your family finances

- A personalized, written eating plan—the best planning tool you can possibly create

Oh, and if the word *budget* really bothers you that much (some people prefer *eating plan* to *diet*), change it. Give it whatever name works for you (a financial plan or family money plan, perhaps, or else let your kids name it), but accept that you'll need to create one, and to follow it. And then get started!

Benefits of a Budget

- You'll know where you stand. No more guesswork as to whether or not you can afford something.

- No more late or avoided payments. Bills will be paid on time and you won't dread phone calls or mail delivery anymore.

- You'll "find" extra money when you stop paying those hidden fees and late payment fees.

- You'll have a visible road map leading you toward your goals.

- You'll be more organized and efficient. No more hours spent searching through desk or kitchen drawers for a receipt in order to return an item, or spent pulling together necessary papers at tax time.

STEP ONE

The best and most basic approach to creating your first budget is to *write everything down* for one entire month. Everything. Every cent that leaves your pocket, purse, wallet, bank account, or cheque book. No exceptions.

That means every cup of coffee on the way to work, every bus trip, every quart of milk, every tip in a restaurant—even the money that you spend on the little notebook that you're going to write it all down in. Carry that little notebook with you everywhere, and get one for your partner, too. Create as many categories in it as you need:

• Groceries

• Insurance

• Utilities

• Entertainment (Be specific. Was it a video rental? Late fees for the movie you forgot to return? A theatre ticket?)

• Transportation

• Child care

• Gifts

• Restaurants

• School activities

• Whatever else you can think of

If you buy something that doesn't fit one of your categories, create a new one. (See Appendix "A" for an example of a budget form called an "Income and Expense Statement.")

STEP TWO

At the end of the month, sit down with your partner and tally the results. If you're like most people, it's quite possible that you'll be shocked at the difference between what you *think* you spend and what you actually *do* spend. Maybe it's the office lunches that have added up to more than what you expected, or maybe the number of times you've given in to your kids' demands for fast food. But whatever the excess is, at least now you know about it, and you've taken your first step towards setting up your tracking system.

You can't relax just yet, however, because you still have some work ahead of you. Now that you know exactly where your hard-earned dollars are going, you need to decide if that's where you *want* them to be going.

STEP THREE

Divide your expenses up into two main categories, fixed and variable. Your fixed expenses will include:

- Mortgage/rent
- Loan payments
- Utilities
- Child support/alimony
- Vehicle payments
- Insurance premiums
- Any other monthly expense that you must pay whether you like it or not

Your variable expenses will include:

• Groceries

• Clothes

• Entertainment

• Home repairs

• Vehicle upkeep

• Books, magazines, and newspapers

• Vacations

• Savings

• Debt repayment

• Periodic expenses like vehicle registration and school fees that come up every so often during the course of the year

• Any other expenses that you have some control over

SUCCESS TIP

Even your fixed payments may have some flexibility. Think about refinancing your home to reduce your mortgage payment if there is equity in the property, or the amortization period could be extended. Or, consider lowering your payments by getting a consolidation loan (more about that in Chapter 4).

STEP FOUR

Once you've categorized everything, it's time to involve the rest of the family—let them see the facts and figures for themselves, and invite their suggestions about making cuts in the variable part of your budget. Not only will they be learning valuable planning and financial skills, but any child (or partner, for that matter) will be a lot more cooperative about making changes if it's his or her own idea, and not one simply imposed by the powers that be.

How Do Your Expenses Measure Up?

According to national guidelines, a family's net income should be allocated as follows:

Shelter	30 per cent
Food	30 per cent
Transportation	10 per cent
Clothing	8 per cent
Savings	5 per cent
Insurance	4 per cent
House/vehicle repairs	5 per cent
Health care	4 per cent
Recreation	4 per cent

You should be spending no more than 20 per cent of your disposable (net) monthly income to repay your consumer debts (not including your mortgage). Anything above that is a sign of financial difficulty.

STEP FIVE

Your final step is to turn your facts, figures, and ideas into an actual plan. This might seem like a lot of work, but if you see it through, you'll be amazed at your new sense of focus and control over your family finances.

In Chapter One, I had you do an income and expense comparison (Appendix "A"). If you did a thorough job then, you should have a total annual income figure that you can use. Divide that figure by 12, and your result will be your average monthly income.

From that income, you must meet all of your fixed expenses first (including the periodic ones). Whatever is left after these expenses becomes available for your variable expenses.

Finding Your Average Monthly Income

Divide your annual net income (after taxes, Employment Insurance, and Canada Pension Plan) by 12. For example, an annual net income of $52,000 divided by 12 would be a monthly net income of $4,333.33.

How you spend the variable portion of your budget is entirely up to you. There is no one right way to do it (in spite of what your well-meaning relatives and friends may try to tell you). This is *your* budget, and if it's going to succeed, then *you* are the one (along with your immediate family, of course) who needs to be able to live with it. As long as it works for you and your family, it is the right budget. Remember those goals and priorities you discussed with your family in Chapter One? Here's where you find out which of those goals is realistic, and which might have to be re-categorized as a longer-term dream.

SUCCESS TIP

Don't look for positive reinforcement for your efforts from other people. Chances are that you'll get a financial horror story instead—not what you need to hear, and certainly not inspiring.

The only people your budget has to work for is YOUR family!

Here is also where your ability to tell the difference between a need and a want becomes critical. Maybe a budding musical genius in the family has been nagging you about violin lessons—is this a need or want? Do you have debts that you must pay down first? Can your musical genius do something to help find the necessary funds? Perhaps he or she is old enough to start planning menus and making up grocery lists in order to trim the food bill. Again, make sure you keep your family involved in the decision-making process. Their cooperation is essential to your success, and it can also make your life a *lot* easier!

Try to plan for every conceivable expense, whether you expect it to come up in the next month or not. Junior might not need any new clothes right this minute, but with winter around the corner, you're looking at a new snowsuit soon (or summer running shoes, or fall raincoat and boots...). By setting aside money each month for a clothing budget, you're covered no matter what—or when—the need. Ditto for other expenses, like prescription drugs, family gifts, home repair, vehicle repair and maintenance, and so on.

SUCCESS TIP

Don't try to do your entire budget all at once. Take a few days, or even weeks if you need to. Break the work down into manageable pieces:

- Gather your income information.
- Gather your expense information (over several days, or weeks, if needed).

- Use a calculator and review your totals.
- Divide your expenses into fixed and variable.
- Make the necessary adjustments.
- Create your plan.

Dietary First Aid

Sometimes, despite your very best efforts, your finished budget still won't balance. Expenses still outweigh income, and lowering your financial stress levels seems more elusive than ever. What do you do?

First of all, don't panic. If your income isn't meeting your expenses, you have three possible solutions:

1. Decrease your expenses

2. Increase your income

3. A combination of both

Let's look at decreasing your expenses first. It's common knowledge—and common sense—that if you want to lose weight you have to give up, or at least drastically cut back on, certain foods, such as sweets and fast foods. A budget diet is no different: Luxury items, such as cigarettes, lottery tickets, beer, and alcohol, will blow the household budget every time. If you haven't already cut these items from your financial plan, now is a great time to do so.

Other things to consider doing are:

• Clipping coupons

• Planning meals around weekly specials

• Shopping at thrift or consignment stores (you can resell your kids' outgrown clothing at the same consignment stores)

• brown-bagging work and school lunches

• borrowing books from the library rather than purchasing them (videos and CDs too!)

Math Facts

A $7 per day savings on lunches adds up to about $1,800 per year!

Personal "Rewards" Program

Even if you've accomplished a balanced budget (your income exceeds your expenses), you can still reduce or cut out your luxury items. Start your own "rewards program" with your savings.

If you save $10 a week by not buying lottery tickets, take your partner out to dinner once a month. Celebrate your budgetary success by using the opportunity to review your goals and plans.

Keep rewards in perspective, however. If you're saving a bundle, don't blow it all on dinners out. Rather, put some of it into RRSP, RESP, or savings accounts (for a vacation, maybe?).

If your expenses still outweigh your income after reviewing your budget and making any changes that you can, your other alternative is to increase your income. Your options here are somewhat limited, but depending on your circumstances you might consider these ideas:

• Getting a part-time job

• Having a stay-at-home spouse or partner find a part-time job

• Renting out a room in your home to a student or boarder

• Selling any assets you own (antiques, stocks, bonds, unused household items) that are fully paid for and not being used as security for a debt that you owe

> **SUCCESS TIP**
>
> If you don't want the hassle of selling an item yourself, take it to a consignment shop and let them handle the selling process. Just remember that they'll keep a commission from the sale price.

And if you've considered all of your options and still can't solve your financial crunch? Get help. Don't let embarrassment stand in your way. Think about what's at stake (your family relationships, your home, your credit rating), and contact a credit counselling agency to set up an appointment—they help people just like you every day, regardless of income level.

> **Remember: ANYONE can get credit counselling!**

Putting Your Budget to Work

Theoretically, your budget should work as well in real life as it does on paper. Sometimes, however, you may still find that you're having trouble following through with it. Keeping track of your personal cash flow is a major task in itself, and with your many different payments and their due dates, it can be a real headache. One way to ease your "pain" is with a paycheque planner.

The simplest way to set up a paycheque planner is with a blank sheet of paper, a pencil, and an eraser. Across the top of the page, list all your net income amounts and the dates they'll be received. You should have something that looks like this:

You: 1st Friday	Your Partner: 15th	You: 3rd Friday	Child Benefit: 28th	Your Partner: 30th

The next step is to slot in your fixed expenses under the appropriate paycheque, according to when they're due. For example, if your partner is paid on the 30th of every month and your mortgage is due on the first, then you would assign the mortgage payment to the 30th's paycheque. If utility payments are due on the 10th of the month, then your first Friday paycheque would be used to pay those. Don't forget to include your periodic payments (such as vehicle insurance), or the amount you need to save each month for those payments, into your planner as well.

Once you've entered your fixed payments, add in your variable expenses, such as transportation, groceries, debt-reduction, savings, etc.). Try to divide these expenses evenly between your paycheques if you can. For instance, if you're paid bi-weekly, allot half your monthly food budget to each of your cheques. This way your standard of living will remain at the same level for the entire month (balanced eating versus feast and famine), and you'll be establishing a routine that will help your entire budget succeed.

Finally, balance your planner. Add up your expenses in each column and compare them to the paycheque to which they've been assigned. If you have shortfall in one column, see if you can move one or more of the expenses there into a column where you have an excess (now you know why you're doing this in pencil, and why you need an eraser!).

Keep fine tuning your figures until you've reached a balance in every column, and your budget will no longer be theoretical...it will be real, practical, workable, and ready to change your financial future.

A Final Word About Budgets

Is a budget fun? You probably won't think so, especially not at first. But once you begin to see your progress (ever-decreasing credit card balances, perhaps?) and feel its other benefits (nothing beats the satisfaction of spending money—guilt free—that you've saved for something), you'll wonder how you ever survived as long as you did without one.

Try to see your budget as *planning* for your priorities and your future, rather than depriving yourself of them, and don't be afraid to revise things as you go along. Remember that this is *your* plan, based on *your* needs (and yes, your wants, too), and that it's not carved in stone.

A truly workable budget, one that you can live with, will take some fine tuning. You're trying to keep your spending within the limits you've set for yourself, but along the way you may find that you've underestimated in some areas and overestimated in others. If that's the case, don't be afraid to make the necessary adjustments.

And finally, be patient! You didn't get into your current financial situation overnight, and you won't get out of it in that time frame, either. It may take a few months to see the results of your work, but you *will* see results—I promise!

CHAPTER SUMMARY

- See the benefits of a budget.
- Build a five-step budget
    - Write down everything that you spend for a month.
    - Tally your results.
    - Categorize your expenses.
    - Balance expenses and income.
    - Create a personalized financial "eating plan."
- Put your budget to work with your paycheque planner.

CHAPTER FOUR

Taming the Scale

Steps to Reducing Your Debt

*"Some people use one half their ingenuity to get into debt,
and the other half to avoid paying it."*
—George D. Prentice

When it comes to designing a debt-reduction plan, your current debt situation will determine the action you need to take. Obviously, if you're facing a drastic problem, then a drastic remedy is needed. If you're currently solvent, however, and only trying to avoid trouble in the first place, then you can create a less extreme "reducing plan."

Regardless of how you're tipping the scale at the moment, one of the first things you need to look at is your current credit rating. Many people who come into my office have a primary goal of maintaining their credit rating. Unfortunately, by the time they involve a specialist like myself, it is usually too late and their credit records already have been severely tarnished.

The best way to ensure that you keep track of your credit rating, and that you deal immediately with any problems or inaccuracies that arise, is to understand what a credit report is and to regularly review yours.

CREDIT REPORT BASICS

Before a lender hands over money to a potential borrower, they want to know (as best they can) whether or not the borrower can be trusted to repay the loan. Lenders base such decisions on a borrower's past credit history—whether or not they've had court judgments against them, if they've ever been bankrupt, how well they pay their current obligations, and so on. This credit history is recorded by a credit bureau. There are two major bureaus in Canada, Equifax Canada and Trans Union of Canada, that provide your credit history to lenders and other creditors (stores, businesses, etc.) for a fee.

In addition to your credit history, a credit bureau will also have information such as your name, current address, birth date, social insurance number, employment history, and information regarding your partner. Credit bureau files also list other creditors who have requested your report, along with the date requested. Files are updated every 30 days.

In order to have a credit rating, you must have either borrowed money or bought goods or services on credit. If you've made your payments on time, you'll have a good credit rating. If you've failed to do so, your report will show you as being in arrears. Should you stop making your payments for a long enough time, you will be classified as being in default.

Understanding Credit Ratings					
Manner of Payment	**Rating**				
	0	**R**	**I**	**C**	**M**
Too new to rate; approved but not used	0	0	0	0	0
Pays (or paid) within 30 days of due date; not more than one payment past due	1	1	1	1	1
Pays (or paid) in more than 30 days, but not more than 60 days or two payments past due	2	2	2	2	2

Manner of Payment	Rating				
	O	R	I	C	M
Pays (or paid) in more than 60 days, but not more than 90 days or three payments past due	3	3	3	3	3
Pays (or paid) in more than 90 days, but not more than 120 days or four payments past due	4	4	4	4	4
Account is at least 120 days overdue, but not yet rated "9"	5	5	5	5	5
Making regular payments under a consolidation order or similar arrangement	7	7	7	7	7
Repossession (voluntary or involuntary return of merchandise)	8	8	8	8	8
Bad debt; placed for collection; skip; bankruptcy	9	9	9	9	9

O = Open account (30 or 90 days)
R = Revolving or option (open-ended account)
I = Instalment (fixed number of payments)
C = Line of Credit
M = Mortgage

How to Check Your Report

You can obtain a copy of your credit bureau report at no charge by contacting Equifax Canada (www.equifax.ca or 1-800-465-7166) or Trans Union of Canada (www.tuc.ca or 1-877-713-3393 in Quebec, 1-866-525-0262 elsewhere in Canada). You can send them a letter, call them for a mail-in request form, or download a form online. If you choose to go online, be careful that you are obtaining the free request form, and not paying for one of their other report services unless you wish to do so!

If you are sending a request by letter, be sure to provide two pieces of personal identification (e.g., photocopy of a driver's licence, bank statement, or utility bill). I recommend providing a copy of one photo ID with your signature on it, so that your signature can be verified. Be sure to sign the letter, or your request may be rejected.

The Importance of Review

Mistakes happen in every business, and credit bureaus are no different. Generally speaking, if wrong information is inserted into your file, it's because that information was given to the bureau by a credit grantor. If one of those mistakes has found its way into your file, you want to know about it and clear it up *before* you find yourself unexpectedly turned down by a lender. Otherwise, you could find yourself in a position like Fred's.

When Fred and his wife wanted to purchase new furniture, they decided to take advantage of the store's don't pay for two years promotion. Unfortunately, when Fred applied for the credit, he was turned down because of several judgments showing on his credit report. Fred, who had never had any judgments against him, requested clarification from the credit bureau and discovered that information about someone with a similar name had been wrongly placed in his file.

To ensure that you're not the victim of this kind of error, you need to review your bureau report regularly to make sure that the information they have on your file is accurate. And, while credit information is generally shared between the reporting services, it's a good idea to request your report from *both* agencies just to be sure.

Fixing Mistakes

If you do find a mistake, contact *both* credit bureaus to have the error corrected as soon as possible. Once you complain to them, they must contact the creditor who provided the information, and request backup information. If the creditor doesn't reply to the request within 30 days, the bureau will usually remove the negative information from your file.

Jennifer, a client of mine, discovered that her credit report held negative information about a credit card that she never had. I contacted the credit bureau and asked them to provide me with a copy of the signed application from the credit card company, and they in turn requested the information from the card issuer. The card company replied that they could not provide the application, and the derogatory mark was immediately removed from Jennifer's file.

Fixing errors in your credit report can be time consuming and frustrating, but it can be done. If you decide to hire people who claim they can repair your credit report, do so with caution. Those who claim they can repair your credit bureau report for a large upfront fee most likely are scam artists. Ask for qualifications and a step-by-step description of what they will do to repair your report, and *do not* pay a hefty fee up front.

Once your credit bureau reports are repaired, get copies of them for your records, and then request your reports every one to two years to make sure that no more errors are made.

If you run into a situation where you have a problem with a creditor who refuses to change a negative report, you have the right to place up to 100 words of explanation on your bureau files. That way, when a creditor looks at the report, they'll be able to see both sides of the story—unless, that is, they're using the new, widespread credit scoring system.

CREDIT SCORING

Initially introduced as a guide to help point out weaknesses in a credit application, credit scoring has largely replaced a creditor's personalized decision regarding whether or not to extend credit. The credit scoring system uses computer technology to assign a numerical valuation based on your credit performance and potential lending risk. Factors that influence your score include income, length of time in your current home, and credit and employment histories.

While the system is certainly more efficient for lenders, computers are not equipped to take extenuating circumstances into consideration—and that could mean an unjust decision for you. For instance, no matter how good your credit rating might be, if you're laid off from your job and are unable to meet your payments for a few months until you find new employment and re-establish yourself, the computer could potentially score you the same as it would someone who is employed but habitually late with his or her payments.

Some creditors will allow a review of a credit file. If you think your circumstances are such that your credit score should be re-evaluated, don't be afraid to discuss the situation with your lender.

CREDIT REPORT CARD QUIZ:
True or False?

- **Credit bureaus determine your credit rating.**
  False: They only record what's reported to them by your creditors.

- **If you apply for too many credit cards or apply for credit too often within a short period of time, you can lose points under the credit scoring system.**
  True: Each time you apply for a new credit card or apply for credit, it's noted on your credit bureau report. Do so too many times in a short period, and it sends up a red flag indicating that you may be overextended.

- **Your credit rating cannot be changed.**
  False: You can have incorrect information changed. Your report will also reflect improved payment habits over time.

- **Negative information will never be removed from your credit report.**
  False: Negative information generally remains on your report for six to seven years.

- **If you owe money to a finance company, it could affect how other creditors view your report.**

True: The fact that you're willing to pay such a high interest rate (28 per cent or more) could mean that you can't get the money from a financial institution. Be aware, however, that some retailers sell their accounts receivable to finance companies who in turn collect those receivables.

- **All your creditors report to the credit bureaus.**
  False: While most creditors do report to the credit bureaus, they are not required to do so.

- **A bankruptcy only shows on your credit bureau report for six years.**
  False: Bankruptcy remains on your record for at least seven years; if it's your second bankruptcy, it's there for 14 years.

- **A lack of credit history is viewed as negative.**
  True: Creditors want some kind of reassurance that you can be trusted to repay them. If you don't have a credit rating, you need to build one.

- **Creditors are wary if you are always near your credit card spending limit.**
  True: In spite of the fact that the credit card companies themselves would like you to be at your limit (more interest for them!), the over-extension spectre haunts your other creditors.

DEALING WITH COLLECTION AGENCIES: KNOW YOUR RIGHTS

Collectors. If you've had the pleasure of dealing with them, you know that it's no pleasure at all. If you haven't, then trust me...you *don't* want to go there.

Collection agents have been described as the "pit bulls of the financial world"—far too accurate a description for comfort. Don't get me wrong, there are collectors out there who are reasonable and ethical. However, there are many others who are not. Too many, in fact, seem unaware of (or simply ignore) provincial laws that prohibit them from harassing or unreasonably threatening debtors. One client called me from her cellphone, while her house telephone rang in the background. A collection agent was trying to collect money from her that she simply didn't have. When I spoke to the collector and told him that he could not continue to make harassing phone calls in the province of Ontario, he laughed and replied that he wasn't in Ontario, so he could do whatever he wanted. The only way my client could get any peace was to unplug her telephone!

Know Your Rights!

A collection agency CAN:

- Contact your friends, employer, relatives, or neighbors to get your address or telephone number
- Contact anyone who has co-signed a debt for you if you haven't paid that debt
- Contact your employer to confirm employment or about a payment connected with a wage assignment (garnishment) or court order

A collection agency CANNOT:

- Try to collect a debt from you without first letting you know, in writing, that it has been assigned to the account
- Take legal action without notifying you and getting your creditor's written permission
- Make harassing phone calls to you or your family (either in tone or in frequency)
- Swear at you
- Threaten you with violence, repossession, or jail time
- Call you on a Sunday, statutory holiday, or before 7 a.m. or after 9 p.m. any other day
- Demand payment of a debt without telling you the name of the creditor and the amount you owe
- Continue to demand payment from you if you don't owe the money
- Give misleading information about you to anyone (such as your employer) that might damage you or your family

Credit collectors work on commission that they receive when you pay the money you owe; the sooner you pay that money, the higher their commission. Consequently, their demands are sometimes ridiculous, like when they wanted another of my clients to pay $15,000 within 48 hours or else they threatened to garnish his wages.

The truth is that a collector can't arbitrarily garnish anyone's wages. Like anyone else seeking to collect, they must proceed through the courts, where you have a chance to defend yourself and tell your side of the story. Only when, and if, they obtain judgment can they garnish your wages.

Just as with credit bureau reports, mistakes can be made by collectors too, and you may find yourself the target of calls for a debt you know nothing about. If you receive harassing phone calls about such an alleged debt, ask the collector to provide you with written particulars. If they refuse to do so, tell them you have no intention of paying a debt you know nothing about, and invite them to sue so that you'll have a right to review the papers.

Collection Agency Violations

In Canada, the actions of collection agencies are policed through the various provincial collection agency acts. If you think an agency is violating the law, you can contact your provincial consumer protection agency. A list is included in Appendix "D" at the end of this book.

Another reason to want to review the documentation is that collectors can, sometimes knowingly, try to collect on a debt that is statute-barred (they've missed the limitation period for collection). Again, if they refuse to provide you with the information, issue an invitation to sue. At least in court you know that your rights will be upheld; and in the meantime, you'll get the collection agents to back down from their bullying tactics.

Negotiating with a Collection Agent

When you deal with a collector, you are in negotiations with them, and whether you realize it or not, your position is the stronger one even if you owe the money. Collectors need you to pay your debt in order for them to get their commission. That said, however, it's important that you try to cooperate with a collector as much as possible. The following do's and don'ts will help:

- **Don't** avoid collectors when they call. This will only frustrate them and make them less likely to listen to you or try to reach a settlement with you.

- If they try humiliation or bullying tactics, **don't** fall into that trap...and **don't** argue.

- **Do** hear them out and understand that they're just trying to do their job.

- Once they've finished, **do** be upfront with them. Be honest and forthright, and explain your side of the story if it differs from theirs.

- If what they say about the debt is true (you owe the money), **do** admit it. Like it or not, you have an obligation to pay the debt.

- If there is a reason you can't pay the debt (job loss, illness, or some other valid reason beyond your control), **do** explain this to the collector. Try to reach a satisfactory settlement with them. Can you send them a cheque for part of the debt now and make another instalment next month? Can you postpone payment for the next two months if you send them a series of postdated cheques now for after that?

- **Do** put any agreement that you reach into writing so that both parties, you and the collector, know each other's rights and obligations.

- If you can't reach an agreement, **don't** just ignore the collector or their demands. Ask them to send the papers to you so that you can deal with the matter appropriately.

• If they aren't willing to send you the information, **do** encourage them to sue you. Even if you owe the money, once your case is before small claims court, you'll have a chance to indicate your ability (or lack thereof) to pay the debt and to reach a payment agreement with your creditor.

Dealing with collectors can be very difficult and intimidating. If, even with the information provided here, you're still not comfortable dealing with a collector on your own, you can retain a professional to do so on your behalf. In some cases I have dealt with, a collector has been more reasonable and cooperative with me than they would have with my client simply because I've had no negative history with that collector.

And speaking of history, if you're avoiding dealing with a collector because you're afraid of damaging your credit rating, you might as well stop worrying. Once your debt hits the collection stage, your credit rating is already severely damaged. The best thing you can do now is deal with the collector and find a way to pay the debt. Only then can you begin work on rebuilding your credit rating.

CHOOSING A DIET PLAN: DEBT-REDUCTION STRATEGIES

You now have a good grasp of the basics of healthy finances: You have your budget in hand, you've set goals for yourself, you've stopped adding to your debt load, you know where you stand with your credit rating, and you're ready to begin. But how?

While there aren't quite as many ways to reduce debt as there are diet plans in the world, you do still have some choices about what works best for you and your family. A lot will depend on how far into the debt hole you are, and whether or not you feel able (disciplined enough) to pull yourself out on your own. The following options might work for you if you're still solvent.

Consolidation Loans

In today's world, it's all too easy to find yourself juggling multiple debts. You start out innocently enough, of course, with one or two credit cards and maybe a car loan. Then a furniture store advertises a don't-pay-for-a-year event, so you get the new couch you've been wanting. You follow this a few months later with a new washer and dryer through an appliance store's interest-free, no-payments-for-six-months promotion. Then a major department store offers you a discount if you apply for their store card, and pretty soon you have a significant debt of convenience on that, too.

Chances are you'll probably manage to stay afloat until the furniture and appliance loans—each at a whopping 32.9 per cent interest rate—come due. And then the trouble starts. The payments are high. Some of them are *very* high. You look to your existing credit cards, or apply for another, for cash advances to meet the payments. And you start losing sleep.

A consolidation loan, where you combine all of your debts into one, with a single monthly payment at a much lower rate of interest than most of your current debts, is one potential debt-diet solution.

Example

Credit card $5,000@ 18.9% = $945

Retail store $4,000 @ 28.8% = $1152

Overdraft $3,000 @ 18% = $540

Total Interest per year - $2,637

Consolidation loan: $12,000 @ 8% = $960

Savings of $1,677 in interest a year

To improve their own bottom lines, financial institutions are currently discouraging small loans of less than $10,000 in favour of credit lines (less paperwork for them means fewer employees and lower over-head costs).

SUCCESS TIP

Whether you're looking at a loan or a credit line, shop around for the best inter-est rate. If you have a long-term relationship with your own financial institution, tell them where you found the best rate and see if they'll better it or match it for you.

For loan amounts greater than $10,000, the loan may be unse-cured, or secured against collateral; it can also have a fixed or vari-able interest rate.

Once you get the consolidation loan, follow through. Pay off the debts that you agreed to consolidate; do not spend the proceeds of the consolidation loan on something else, or your debt waistline will begin to bulge all over again.

Lines of Credit

A line of credit is a pre-set, maximum amount of money that you can borrow from a lender. Like a loan, it can be secured against your home, vehicle, cottage, bonds, or other collateral, or it can be unse-cured. An unsecured credit line will have a lower borrowing limit than a secured one, usually in the range of $5,000 to 15,000. The amount you can borrow on a secured credit line will vary according to how much equity you have in your home, or how much your col-lateral is worth.

Home Equity

Not sure how much equity you have in your home? Try checking local real estate listings for similar properties. If that doesn't help, you can get an appraisal done by a qualified real estate appraiser—you may even be able to provide your lender with the appraisal, although the lender may want a second, independent opinion. The average cost of an appraisal can vary between $300 and $600 plus GST.

A line of credit has many benefits: You can draw from it at any time (up to the pre-set limit) and use it for anything you want. You pay interest only when you use the money, and only on the amount that you actually borrow. You may be able to make interest-only payments if your funds happen to be a little tight some months, and there are no credit checks every time you want to use the line of credit.

Interest rates on a credit line are generally lower than loan rates—prime plus one to two percent for a secured line, and prime plus four to five percent for an unsecured line—and they fluctuate according to the prime rate. You may also be able to lock in your interest rate if the prime rate climbs too high for comfort; talk to your lender about this option.

While you might initially take out a line of credit in order to consolidate your other debts, once you've paid it down it can provide another function as well—that of an emergency fund. Instead of trying to save two to three months' salary, and putting yourself and your family into a financial pinch, your line of credit can be a cost-effective way to deal with the unexpected (a new roof, major vehicle repairs, etc.). But don't fall into the trap of using the credit line for other things (those sneaky wants, for example), or you'll find yourself right back where you started!

SUCCESS TIP

Increase your odds of obtaining a loan or credit line by checking your credit report in advance and dealing with any inaccuracies you find.

If you're a contract worker, or expect your employment to terminate sometime in the future (at which point you would no longer qualify for the credit), a credit line can see you through your transition time, and you can pay it down again once you're employed. Just remember, apply for the line of credit while you are still working, instead of when you are no longer employed.

Should you reach a point where you no longer want to have a line of credit, you can do one of two things:

• If you don't currently owe money on the credit line and firmly believe that you won't ever need it again, simply request that the financial institution close it out.

• If you do still owe money, but no longer want access to additional funds (as a spending control, perhaps), ask your financial institution to terminate the credit line and convert it into a loan with set monthly payments.

Assets: Finding Your Hidden Dollars

A client came into my office one day complaining that she could no longer afford to pay her bills because she simply didn't have enough money. When we reviewed her financial situation, however, I found that she had an art collection worth between $75,000 and $100,000 and a silver collection valued at $50,000. Astonishingly, this woman honestly believed that she had no money—and she's not alone in her misguided mindset.

Many people who consider themselves poor, or believe that they have no money, are really only *cash-flow poor*. They may actually have a great deal of net worth on paper, but without enough ready cash to spend, they end up scrimping from day to day, trying to figure out how to pay next month's bills. Assets that they may not have considered include equity in their home, RRSPs, inherited collections, artwork, and much more.

SUCCESS TIP

Use assets to improve your (and your family's) life, especially if finances are causing stress. Your children would much rather experience family harmony now than inherit great-grandma's silver when you're gone.

Unfortunately, their belief in their poverty will reflect back onto them and the way that they and their families live. It will cause unnecessary stress, friction within the family regarding spending habits, and reduced enjoyment in life in general. If your financial reality is such that you need to reduce your debt load or else face serious consequences (such as collection agencies, a damaged credit rating, or bankruptcy), then you owe it to yourself and your family to take a second look at your net worth and see if your assets can be used to alleviate some of your debt pressure.

Start by thinking about what you can sell. Assets are really money in disguise. Some appreciate, some depreciate. The appreciating ones are your opportunity to "cash in" on some badly needed cash.

Do you still get the same pleasure from your art collection as you did when you began to acquire the pieces? Or are you faced with additional security costs for your home and increased insurance premiums, neither of which you can really afford? Do you really need that summertime-only sports car or is it causing friction between you and your partner/spouse because it's worth enough to significantly pay down the family's debts?

What about your home? If your kids have moved out, do you really need to keep that four-bedroom house with its taxes, insurance premiums, and general maintenance? Even if you want enough space for the kids to stay when they come to visit, is it worth the financial overload you're facing? Maybe a smaller, more modest home will do just as well, saving you both money and time on its upkeep.

Reducing your cost of living is a priority if you find yourself strapped for cash on a monthly basis. Remember, keeping up with the Joneses is *not* what your life is or should be all about!

As a last resort, if you're really in a cash squeeze or faced with an emergency, you can withdraw money from your RRSP or an RESP to see you through a difficult time. If you go the RRSP route, you'll lose the ability for your RRSP to grow quickly, and you'll end up paying tax on the amount you withdraw. If you collapse an RESP (not something I recommend, but an available option nonetheless), you'll get back your contributions, but you won't receive any of the interest you've earned. (For more information on RRSPs and RESPs, see Chapter Ten.)

If you're holding funds in trust for your child in a non-registered education savings plan, you can cash it in or borrow against it. Please remember, however, that you have both a legal and a moral obligation to repay the funds.

REBUILDING (OR BUILDING) A CREDIT HISTORY

Once you're on the road to successful debt reduction, you also need to recover from your blemished credit past. To do this, you need to build a credit bureau history that shows you can be relied on to meet your obligations as they come due. (The tips here also apply to someone just beginning to build a credit history.)

Patience and understanding will be your best friends in accomplishing this feat. Starting over (or starting out) will take time, and with a bad (or no) history behind you, lenders will understandably view you with a more critical eye.

Loans

One of the best ways to begin to build or rebuild your credit history is to borrow a small amount of money and make regular payments on time, even if you can afford to pay off the entire amount at once. Of course, because you don't *have* a reliable credit history, trying to find a lender willing to help you out is a little like being caught between a rock and a hard place.

Finance companies are more likely to lend money to high-risk clients than banks or credit unions are (at 28 per cent to 33 per cent interest, they can afford the additional risk). As unpalatable as paying the high rates may seem, it may still be worthwhile to borrow a small amount (say $1,000) and make regular payments for six to eight months before paying off the balance in full. You won't have paid too big a fortune in interest, and you'll have taken your first step to re-establishing yourself as a reliable debtor.

If you prefer to deal with a bank or credit union, first open a substantial savings account (let's say $1,000 again). For a few months, add to the savings on a fairly regular basis, then apply for a loan of an amount less than what you have in your account, and use the account as security. Again, make your payments for several months before paying off the loan.

Secured Credit Cards

A secured credit card is another way of re-establishing your credit, one that is particularly useful if you do a lot of travelling that requires hotel and car reservations. It works much the same way as a secured loan, but instead of opening a savings account, you pay the money to the credit card company as a security deposit.

Where to Find a Secured Credit Card

While secured credit cards aren't widely available in Canada, Home Trust offers a secured card (1-888-281-7793 or www.hometrust.ca).

The credit card itself is like any other. You can use it in all the same places, and for all the same purposes. Because it is a secured card, however, your credit limit will be no more than the amount you have on deposit with the card company (anywhere from $500 to $10,000). If you default on your payments, your deposit is used to pay off the balance.

Your security deposit earns interest for as long as your credit card account is open and in good standing (up to date). Once you have established a solid credit-repayment history and want to cancel the card, all you have to do is pay the outstanding balance and your security deposit—plus interest—will be returned to you.

CHAPTER SUMMARY

- Credit reports are maintained by reporting organizations, who accumulate information from the organizations you owe money to. Review the reports every couple of years for errors.

- Credit scoring is a method of arriving at a credit rating, but can be ambiguous.

- Collection agencies are hired to obtain outstanding debt payments from you, and receive a portion of that payment as their fee.

- Use debt-reduction strategies

  - Consolidation loans enable you to combine debts into one regular payment.

  - Sale of assets can be a source of cash.

- Rebuilding a credit history takes time and effort, but is worth it.

  - Loans can be obtained to pay off debt, often at a lower rate of interest than you're paying.

  - Secured credit cards let you draw against an amount you've already deposited on the card.

CHAPTER FIVE

Legally Speaking

Serious Options for Serious Debt Disorders

"I finally know what distinguishes man from the other beasts: financial worries."
—Jules Renard

Sometimes a simple diet is not enough to deal with eating habits that have become a more serious problem; the same can be true of our finances. If, despite your best efforts, your financial situation has deteriorated beyond what you can stomach on your own, you may need to take more formal, legal steps to correct your situation—just as you would seek professional help for an eating disorder. Again, your options will vary according to the severity of your financial dysfunction.

ORDERLY PAYMENT OF DEBTS

Some provinces (Alberta, Nova Scotia, Prince Edward Island, and Saskatchewan) have an Orderly Payment of Debts program. This program provides for payment in full of all debts within three to four years. You must, however, meet income and other qualifications before being accepted into the program. Regulations differ from province to province, but the overall process is the same.

Benefits of an Orderly Payment of Debts Program

- Your debts are repaid in full.

- Your interest will be at a fixed rate, usually lower than the going rate.

- Payments are based on your ability to pay.

- You are protected from certain legal actions (such as wage garnishments).

- You avoid bankruptcy.

- You'll no longer receive harassing phone calls or demand letters either at home or at work.

To begin the program, you must see a credit counsellor at an appropriate credit counselling location (see Appendix "C" for a list of locations). The counsellor will help you identify all of your debts and living expenses, and then develop a monthly repayment schedule based on your ability to pay. The counsellor will then apply to the court for a consolidation order under Canada's *Bankruptcy and Insolvency Act* (Note: This does **not** mean that you are bankrupt) and your creditors will have 30 days to file any objections to the plan. Assuming no objections are filed, the order will be approved and you will begin making monthly payments to your credit counselling agency, which in turn distributes the funds to your creditors. As a part of the program, you will also attend budgeting and credit workshops to assist you toward financial success.

A Word of Caution

Only the debts listed in the Orderly Payment of Debts order will be paid through the program. If you take on additional debts after you enter the program, you'll have to see your credit counsellor for additional help or try to pay those debts on your own outside of the program.

The Orderly Payment of Debts program does not work for everyone. Your credit counsellor will be able to advise you regarding the program and any other options you might have.

CONSUMER PROPOSALS

Another option, available to any Canadian resident (including bankrupt individuals), is the Consumer Proposal. This is a proposal you make to your creditors to modify the payment of your debts. For example, you could propose to pay back a percentage of the debt you owe, either in a lump sum, over a period of time, or a combination of both. To qualify for this avenue, you must be a Canadian resident, owe a minimum of $1,000 and a maximum of $75,000 (not including your home mortgage), and be insolvent. A joint proposal can also be made in the case of spouses/partners, in which case total debts cannot exceed $150,000 (not including your home mortgage).

For your proposal to be acceptable to your creditors, it must give them more money than they would get if you filed for bankruptcy. In addition, you must meet one of the following three requirements:

• You are steadily employed at an income level above what you need for normal living expenses.

• A third party is willing to provide the funding for, or guarantee, the proposal.

• You voluntarily offer certain assets that would not be available to creditors if you went bankrupt.

An administrator, usually a trustee in bankruptcy, will oversee your proposal and notify your creditors, who will have 45 days to consider whether they want to accept or reject the proposal. If your creditors do not respond, the proposal is considered accepted. If there is a vote, a simple majority of creditors is sufficient to approve the proposal. It will then be binding on you and all creditors, whether they voted in favour or not.

Benefits of a Consumer Proposal

- You keep your assets (although they'll be taken into consideration when the administrator is determining how much you need to offer to pay creditors).

- You make one payment a month to your administrator, who distributes the funds to the creditors.

- You'll attend two financial counselling sessions to help you understand how you got into financial difficulty, and how to avoid it in future.

- You avoid bankruptcy.

- Your successful completion of a proposal will be recorded in your credit bureau report.

- You'll no longer receive harassing phone calls or demand letters either at home or at work.

Once your proposal is accepted, your unsecured creditors cannot take any further legal steps to recover their debts from you (such as property seizure or wage garnishments) unless the proposal is annulled because of your failure to meet the proposal's terms.

If you follow through on all the terms of your proposal, you will receive a Certificate of Full Performance from your administrator that relieves you of the debts that were covered by your proposal. If you fail to perform your proposal, you will return to the same position you were in before making it (debtor's purgatory). Your creditors can then proceed against you for the amount owed to them before the proposal was filed, less any amount they received during the course of the proposal. If you are bankrupt when the proposal is made and the court subsequently annuls your proposal, you are then bankrupt once again as of the annulment date.

PERSONAL BANKRUPTCY

While bankruptcy discharges you from most of your debts, it also shadows you for years after. You should consider it your last option, only after you've exhausted all other avenues. A bankruptcy trustee will help you decide if this is the right step for you and walk you through the process. The following is an overview of what to expect.

The Bankruptcy Process

Once you decide to declare bankruptcy, your property (with certain exceptions, known in the bankruptcy field as exemptions) is handed over to the trustee, who then sells it and distributes any money received to your creditors. You will have to attend two counselling sessions. In the first, you will learn about money management, spending habits, and responsible use of credit. In the second, you will look at the reasons for your own bankruptcy and establish a rehabilitation program to avoid future financial difficulties.

Your trustee will require a Statement of Affairs from you, listing your assets, liabilities, income, and expenses. You will also have to answer questions regarding family, employment, and the recent disposition of any assets. The trustee will investigate any transactions prior to your bankruptcy that involved the transfer of any of your assets for less than market value, or that may have favoured one creditor over another. If the trustee uncovers any such transactions, legal proceedings will be started to reverse them.

Before You Sign

Even though your legal documents will be prepared by your trustee, you are still responsible for their accuracy. Be sure that you review them and fully understand everything in them before you sign.

Once the paperwork for your bankruptcy is filed with the courts, your creditors have the option of calling a meeting, called a creditors' meeting. If they choose to do so, you must attend and answer their questions. The creditors can also vote to confirm your trustee's appointment, or to substitute one of their choice.

Income Taxes and Bankruptcy

If you have not filed your income tax return for the year or years prior to your bankruptcy, your trustee will do so, along with a pre-bankruptcy return for the current year covering the period from January first until the date of your bankruptcy.

Any income tax refunds that are due for the current and previous years are considered assets of the bankruptcy and will be forwarded by Canada Customs and Revenue Agency (CCRA) to the trustee. If you happen to receive a refund in error, you must forward it to the trustee; if you don't, the trustee can oppose your discharge from the bankruptcy until you repay the amount and you can be charged with a bankruptcy offence, punishable by a fine, imprisonment, or both.

Bankruptcy: An Easy Out?

Some people consider bankruptcy an easy way to get out of their personal debts while concealing assets or failing to disclose certain information. They're wrong! The *Bankruptcy and Insolvency Act* contains measures for dealing with individuals who commit bankruptcy offences—including fines and/or imprisonment of up to three years. Bankruptcy offences include:

- Fraudulently disposing of property
- Failing to comply with duties and responsibilities
- Refusing to answer questions at an examination
- Falsifying accounts or statements
- Concealing, destroying, or falsifying financial books or records

---

- Hiding or removing assets
- Obtaining credit during the bankruptcy period without informing the creditor of the bankruptcy
- Engaging in a trade or business while bankrupt without telling anyone involved in your business transactions about the bankruptcy

---

If you owe taxes for prior year returns and on the pre-bankruptcy return, those taxes become part of the debts that will be discharged in your bankruptcy.

You will be responsible for filing a post-bankruptcy tax return for the remaining part of the current year. It will be due on the same April 30th date of the following year as any other personal return. If you owe any money on your post-bankruptcy return, you will have to pay it. If a refund is owed to you, it will most likely be forwarded to you unless you have assigned it to your bankruptcy trustee, in which case the refund becomes part of the estate.

Your Duties as a Bankrupt

As a bankrupt, it is your duty to become familiar with certain legal responsibilities and obligations, and to make sure you follow through on them. The court doesn't take kindly to bankrupts who claim they didn't know about their duties:

- You must turn over all your assets to the trustee and help the trustee make an inventory of those assets. If you acquire assets during your bankruptcy and your trustee becomes aware of them, the trustee will also take those assets (including lottery winnings and inheritances) for the benefit of your creditors.

- You must give the trustee all of your available financial books and records.

- You must tell the trustee about all property that you've disposed of through sale, gift, or settlement in the year preceding your bankruptcy (five years for real estate transactions).

- You must attend the first meeting of creditors and any other scheduled meetings, if any are called.

- You must attend any examination that the Official Receiver asks you to.

- You must attend at least two counselling sessions.

- You must give the trustee any information needed to file a pre-bankruptcy income tax return.

- You must generally assist the trustee.

- You must tell the trustee if you move, change your phone number, or change jobs.

- You must give the trustee monthly income and expense statements along with your monthly payments and any surplus income payments.

- If you are a director of a company, you must resign. Under both federal and provincial law, an undischarged bankrupt cannot be a corporate director.

- You must turn over all your credit cards to the trustee for cancellation. Keeping any of the cards, even if there is nothing owing on them, is a bankruptcy offence.

Debts Not Released by Bankruptcy

Bankruptcy doesn't discharge you from all of your debts. If you owe any of the following (not all are listed) you will still have to pay, regardless of your bankruptcy:

- Any court fines or restitution orders
- Any debt or liability for alimony and/or child support
- Any award of damages by a court in respect of intentionally inflicted

bodily harm or sexual assault, or wrongful death that results

- Any debt or liability resulting from fraud, embezzlement, or misappropriation while acting in a position of trust
- Debts for obtaining property by false pretences or fraudulent misrepresentation
- Debts for student loans in certain circumstances

Discharge from Bankruptcy

Bankruptcy is intended to give an honest but unfortunate debtor a fresh financial start. If you fit both those categories, are a first-time bankrupt, and have met all of your duties and responsibilities, then you may qualify for an **automatic discharge** after nine months in bankruptcy (unless your discharge is opposed by any creditors, the Superintendent of Bankruptcy, or your trustee).

If you failed to attend either or both of your counselling sessions, didn't pay the required amount into your bankruptcy estate, or chose to file for bankruptcy instead of making a bankruptcy proposal where possible, then your trustee must recommend a conditional discharge with conditions to be set by the court. A conditional order of discharge outlines what you have to do (usually pay a certain amount of money to the trustee) before you can get an absolute discharge. If you're unable to meet the conditions set out, you can apply to the court after one year to have the conditions changed (you'll have to show reasonable probability that the conditions cannot be met).

Other types of discharge orders may be given if your discharge is opposed. If the court finds it appropriate to penalize you for your conduct, or the bankruptcy isn't your first, it could issue a suspended order of discharge, which means that you'll receive your absolute discharge on a specific date in the future. And on rare occasions, if the court finds you undeserving of discharge (e.g., you've had three or more bankruptcies) it could issue a refusal of discharge.

Be sure to follow up with your trustee to make certain that you get your final discharge. If you can't be located or you haven't cooperated with the trustee, your discharge could be delayed indefinitely. If that happens, your trustee can still be discharged and your file closed, leaving you more vulnerable than you were than before the bankruptcy (i.e., creditors can resume their collection procedures for pre-bankruptcy debts).

Life Without Discharge

If your trustee closes your bankruptcy file and you have not received your absolute discharge:

- You remain a bankrupt.
- You cannot obtain credit without advising your creditor(s) of your bankruptcy.
- Creditors can resume collection efforts for pre-bankruptcy debts.
- Any non-exempt assets can continue to be seized.

Your Future After Bankruptcy

Many people are concerned about what bankruptcy will do to their employment/employability. In most cases, it won't affect either. However, if your job requires you to be bonded, you need to contact the bonding company and address any concerns they have. If their concerns relate to the issue of whether or not you can be trusted to properly handle money, you may be able to alleviate their worries by explaining the cause of your bankruptcy. A bankruptcy caused by layoff or disability, for example, is very different from one triggered by gambling or credit misuse.

Bankruptcy, when used properly, is an invaluable tool for helping honest yet unfortunate people find their way out of otherwise impossible financial situations. It is not a miracle pill for instant debt-weight loss; nor is it intended to function as a yo-yo diet (gain a little debt-weight here, go bankrupt to lose it, then gain it back again). Regardless of your reasons for choosing the bankruptcy route—loss of employment, credit misuse, or whatever—it's your responsibility to take the steps needed to make sure you never have to take the same route again. Educate yourself, educate your family, get the help you need, and build your financial future with as much care and attention as it, and your family, deserves.

CHAPTER SUMMARY

- The Orderly Payment of Debts program has a number of benefits, including avoiding bankruptcy.

- Consumer Proposals enable you to avoid bankruptcy by arranging payment that nets the creditors more than they would receive if you go bankrupt.

- Personal bankruptcy is a last option.

  - There is a very defined process.

  - As a bankrupt, you must fulfill certain duties.

  - There are several levels of discharge from bankruptcy.

  - You must take steps to ensure you return to a more financially responsible life after bankruptcy.

CHAPTER SIX

Staying on Track

Purchasing and Spending Strategies

*"There was a time when a fool and his money were soon parted,
but now it happens to everybody."*
—Adlai E. Stevenson

Impulses…the potential downfall of every dieter. That triple-fudge mega-sundae can sabotage the very best of intentions when you're trying to lose weight—and suddenly the world is *full* of triple-fudge mega-sundaes! Now that you're on a debt diet, you'll be facing many of those impulses yourself (only the sundae will be a television, a vacation, or some other want). So how do you prepare for those challenges?

The Debt Dieter's Golden Rule

Plan, plan, plan! If it isn't planned, and it isn't an emergency, it doesn't get bought!

It's actually a lot easier than you might think. Weight-loss success isn't attained through total deprivation, and neither is debt-loss success. The savvy dieter will build in allowances for the occasional treat now and again. By cutting back on calories at lunch and dinner, an occasional small hot-fudge sundae can be enjoyed guilt free, while staying on track. The savvy debt dieter will follow the same tactic. By sticking to a realistic budget and planning your extras, you can set aside the money you need to enjoy a guilt-free purchase that doesn't knock your debt diet for a complete loop. And because you've literally *earned* the purchase, you'll even enjoy it more!

The trick, of course, is in recognizing the difference between a want and a need (remember Chapter Two?). If you're having difficulty with this differentiation, try giving yourself a cooling-off period. Make a deal with yourself that you'll think about the potential purchase for a week before making a decision. During that week, review your budget and your goals. Can you afford the item? Is this something on your priority list? Does it bring you closer to reaching one of your goals?

Are You a Compulsive Shopper?

Shopping can take on dark overtones for some people. Compulsive, or binge, shopping, is now recognized as an addiction disorder—called oniomania—and it can cause serious damage to a family's finances. If you recognize any of the following signs of compulsive shopping in yourself or someone you love, seek professional help.

- Tending to shop and spend large amounts of money when you're depressed or distressed

- Unable to pass up a "good deal," even when you know you can't afford it

- Arguing with others about your shopping/spending habits, and perhaps lying about what you've bought or spent

- Buying things on credit that you wouldn't have bought if you'd had to pay cash

- Not wearing or using much of what you purchase, and maybe even hiding things from others

- Experiencing a "high" from spending money, and maybe a rush of anxiety at the same time

- Spending money on shopping instead of paying bills
- Shopping interferes with your work or personal relationships

Chances are that at the end of the week you'll have decided that you really don't need the item after all, but if the item still seems important, then perhaps you should try to find a way to purchase it (without credit, of course).

Planning won't make all your wants possible, but it will allow you to incorporate enough of them to make sure that you continue to enjoy life even while your debt is losing weight and your finances are gaining health.

Of course, not all purchases are impulse buys. Some are just plain emergencies, and some are major purchases that we all face eventually (new furniture or appliances, a new vehicle, a home, etc.).

Beware the "Want" in Disguise!

Emergencies are a part of life—your vehicle breaks down, your washer packs it in, your roof springs a leak—and you need to deal with them whether you're prepared or not.

But be careful not to let an emergency need grow into a want. There's a big difference between needing a new fridge (because yours is thawing all over the kitchen floor) and wanting the latest hi-tech, state-of-the-art, several-thousand-dollar model.

So when you're making an emergency purchase, remember to be firm with the salesperson—and yourself—about what you really need.

EMERGENCY PURCHASES

If you're faced with something in the emergency department (like a dead dryer, for instance), be sure you consider all your options. Can your dead dryer be repaired for a reasonable cost? If not, could you buy used instead of new, at least until your cash flow improves?

If you're convinced that your best or only option is to buy new, but you'll have to do so on credit, then look for the best terms you can find. A major credit card will carry a much lower interest rate than a store card will; interest on a bank loan or credit line will be lower still.

You may also have the option of a buy now, pay later offer, but you need to be very cautious here. There are several hidden pitfalls in these schemes that can derail your debt diet in a hurry:

• There is always a minimum purchase value. If you have to buy a more expensive item than what you'd planned on just to meet the minimum limit, then this is a very bad route to take.

• Repayment terms aren't as clear-cut as they seem. This type of financing is actually a loan (usually through a finance company). If you don't repay the full balance at the end of the agreement, interest is chargeable at the full credit account rate beginning at day one of the loan. This is called an acceleration clause.

• If the plan calls for instalments and you've made every one of your payments on time except for the last one, interest may be chargeable on the full amount for the full period.

• Even if there's no interest during the agreed period, you may have to pay other fees and charges (such as financing charges).

Reality Check

• Furniture Purchase—$3,000—No $$ Down—Don't Pay for 2 years

• Scenario #1—on 2 years less a day you pay $3,000—account closed

• Scenario #2—on 2 years plus a day (only one day late) you pay $3,000 plus you also owe interest dating back to the date of purchase (e.g. $3,000 @ 28.9% = $867 per year x 2 years—$1,734 interest)—total cost $4,734

Basically, unless you know for certain that you can pay off the loan within its terms and exactly on time, this is a risky move. If you still want to consider the idea, read the agreement very carefully, and be sure you know what you're letting yourself in for.

MAJOR PURCHASES

Plan. Plan, plan, plan. I can't stress that need enough. Every major purchase that you make in your lifetime should be planned (unless it's an unforeseen emergency). Furniture, appliances, vehicles, houses...all planned.

And when I talk about planning, I mean that an item is included in your goals, that you've specifically set aside money for it, and that you've factored in any debt that you need to incur (e.g., a mortgage). Planning means that you know that this is a want or need that you share with your family, and that you can take on the debt without stressing your budget. In other words, the purchase fits your personal finances.

Furniture/Appliances

If you're planning to buy furniture or major appliances, go back and reread the section about buy now, pay later offers...and then, unless you're extremely confident that you can avoid the pitfalls, don't take that route. Even if you have the money set aside for your new couch and think that you'll earn a few bucks of interest by tucking the money away into an investment until the loan is due, think again. It's all too easy—and it happens all too often—for something unexpected to come up between now and the payoff; you use the couch money to fix the leaky roof, the loan comes due, and suddenly you're stuck with an interest rate of more than 30 per cent. (You don't even want to know what that couch will end up costing you at that rate!)

So play it safe, and smart, and pay cash for your furniture and appliance purchases *after* you've saved for them.

Purchasing a Vehicle

Purchasing a car is often the second biggest financial commitment that people make, which is the first biggest reason that it should be done carefully.

Start by assessing your needs (an upscale SUV for driving to and from work in the city would be a want, not a need). Consider your budget, your driving habits, and how many people you're transporting (if you have three small children and drive across Canada annually to visit family, a two-door compact makes no more sense than that upscale SUV did a moment ago).

New or Used?

You'll also have to think about whether or not you want to, or even should, buy new. You may have heard that a car loses 30 per cent of its value when you drive it off the lot. Unfortunately, the statement isn't that far from the truth. Cars do depreciate rapidly in the first two years, regardless of how well they're maintained or how little they're driven.

It often makes more sense, especially for your finances, to purchase a used vehicle. Most of the newer vehicles come with a minimum five-year warranty, so if you purchase a two-year-old car you still have the advantage of the three remaining years without paying a premium to be the first owner.

Financing

Whether a vehicle is new or used, the cheapest way to purchase it is with cash. You have no interest to pay, and you can often negotiate a better price. However, for the majority of people, financing is needed. Here again, it will pay to shop around. Many dealerships will offer a very low interest rate as an incentive, but as with any other "deal," you'd be wise to read the fine print carefully. What is advertised as zero interest today may only be zero per cent for the first year, after which you're stuck with a sharply increased rate for the remaining time (the average car loan takes five years to pay down). Remember that such a rate increase also means a payment increase—one that might be more than you can comfortably afford.

SUCCESS TIP

When you're thinking of purchasing a vehicle, remember to look beyond the actual price tag. There will be taxes, registration, insurance, and repair costs as well. Make sure that you factor these into your budget before you make your decision.

Leasing

Leasing can make sense for any driver who insists on driving a new vehicle every couple of years, because you're only financing the depreciation of the vehicle over the course of the lease period. Leases also often include servicing costs (with the exception of tires and exhaust systems), giving you further peace of mind. However, as with all contracts, do read the fine print. Pay special attention to details such as mileage limitations, wear and tear, and penalties for breaking the lease.

If you plan to keep the vehicle for more than three or four years, then an outright purchase makes more sense.

Buying a Home

Investing in a home makes excellent sense no matter how you look at it. A house is durable, always saleable, and, for many of us, acts as a forced savings plan. While rent may be cheaper, many people's good intentions about investing what they save (the difference between their rent and what a mortgage payment would be) never amount to anything. And the real bonus, especially come retirement time, is that any gain you make on the sale of your home, provided that it is your principal residence, is tax free.

Financing

To purchase a home, you'll need a minimum of five per cent of the purchase price as a down payment; this leaves 95 per cent of the price to be mortgaged. The same advice applies to finding a mortgagee (lender) as it does to acquiring any service: Shop around, ask questions, and read the fine print. Both mortgage rates and terms vary between lenders, so be sure to talk to more than one. Consider going to a mortgage broker who will do the shopping for you and come back with the best available options and rates.

You'll simplify your search for a home if you pre-qualify for a mortgage before you actually begin looking. A financial institution may have a different idea than you about what you can afford to borrow: Finding out that you can't have the house you've already fallen in love with can be downright demoralizing. (A real estate agent, if you're dealing with one, can give you a rough idea of your pre-qualification, but you should still have your financing pre-arranged.)

If you're planning to purchase a new home from a builder or developer, review the contract conditions carefully, especially with regard to the return of your deposit in case the deal falls through. There have been many cases where people have made large deposits on homes to be built, and then, when they were unable to complete the transaction, they lost their deposit. Have your lawyer review the contract.

A deposit made on an existing home should be made conditional on a satisfactory building inspection. If you find a problem with the house, you'll be able to walk away from the deal unscathed.

PLANNING A VACATION

Vacations...ah, who doesn't dream of golden stretches of sand, tropical skies, crystal clear waters? And with the deals that travel agents offer today, that dream seems so attainable....

Work frustrations and stress can lead even the most well-intentioned soul to throw caution to the wind. Get stuck slogging through mid-February's deep-freeze and before you know it, you've committed that debt diet no-no: You've given in to an impulse. Couple the desire to get away from it all with the instant gratification marketing schemes, and the results can be a lot more expensive than you'd anticipated.

Fly now, pay later is nothing more than another form of credit. And, as you should know by now, credit costs. A lot. Unless you're 300 per cent certain that you can pay off your vacation within its terms, you *cannot* afford to take this route.

Reality Check

A fly now, pay later vacation may not be all it seems. First of all, you will usually have to pay the departure taxes upfront with the balance of the vacation price due later and "later" may mean a maximum of 54 days after your departure date. After which time the entire balance due becomes payable and begins to attract interest at the credit granting facility rate— commonly as high as 28.9%

A vacation should be something that relieves stress—not something that adds to it by creating financial headaches. Make sure that you can afford the holiday that you plan, and don't overlook the cheaper alternatives. Most cities have hostels (year-round) and college dorms (during summer months) that make great alternatives to expensive hotels, and home-swapping is becoming increasingly popular. Travelling off-season can also cut costs, as can making your own meals instead of eating out (even if you're hotelling, you can take along a cooler with snacks and sandwich makings).

Vacation Package Caution!

If you decide to take advantage of a vacation package, be sure you understand what's included. Not all packages are all-inclusive, and people often end up paying for unanticipated extras, including:

- Food, beverages, and entertainment

- Transportation and accommodation costs if your flight leaves from a distant airport

- Air travel departure and arrival taxes, security taxes, airport improvement taxes, etc.

- Transportation from the arrival airport to your accommodation and back again

---

Regardless of where or how you decide to vacation, remember to factor in all the costs. Some of the most frequently overlooked expenses include:

- Exchange rates on currency

- Travel health insurance

- House sitter (check with your home insurance company to be sure that your home is adequately looked after while you're away—your insurance could be invalid if you haven't taken proper precautions)

- Kennel for pets

- Adequate spending money

- Film and developing costs

- Credit carrying costs if you'll be using your credit card for any of your expenses

Like any other purchase, your vacation should be a planned expense. If you set money aside monthly into a special vacation fund until you meet your savings goal, you'll be able to enjoy your well-earned vacation stress-free, with cash and a clear conscience.

HOLIDAY SHOPPING

Christmas is the time for giving. And we Canadians rise to the occasion admirably, getting caught up in the marketing frenzy and using our credit cards freely.

Unfortunately, the downside to this generous spirit is a serious shopping hangover, as evidenced by the trend over the last 10 years with bankruptcies rising between the months of January and April, just as the bills begin rolling in.

But as common as this hangover is, it doesn't have to happen. Once again, the key is planning—realistic planning. Before you even begin your Christmas shopping, review these tips:

1. Check your list—twice. If your list has become unmanageable, try to share the cost of gifts, or divide the list between family members. Some families opt to buy gifts only for the children (nieces, nephews, grandkids); others draw names so that they're purchasing for only one member. Consider exchanging home-baked goodies, and having your kids make their gifts for their teachers.

2. Budget. Know how much you have to spend, set an amount for each gift, and stick to it.

3. Pre-shop. Check out catalogues and stores in advance, jotting down ideas and costs. If you find you're over-budget, keep looking for better prices.

4. Be the early bird. If you sleep in on the weekend, you'll face a loud, overcrowded mall when you arrive to do your shopping. Your budget will go out the window when you buy the first thing that you can lay your hands on, just so you can escape the mayhem.

5. Cash or charge? Pay cash at the till and the price is final. Charge it, and you'll pay up to an additional 28.8 per cent in interest.

6. Plan the payments. See if the store offers an instalment plan: Service charges for these are often cheaper than charge card interest.

7. Buy now, pay later...with extreme caution! Remember that if you can't meet the terms on time, you'll face outrageous interest charges.

8. Think value, not cost. Gift giving should never be about the cost of an item. A simple, but lovingly handcrafted item can mean far more to a recipient than an expensive trinket.

9. Share the joy. For the person who has everything, help out a worthy cause in his/her name.

10. Protect yourself. Gift and credit card thieves love the holidays. Stay alert.

CREDIT TOOLS

Swing a hammer the right way and you can build a house. Swing it carelessly and you'll be nursing a sore thumb for days.

The same common sense rule of thumb holds true for all tools—including the tools of credit (loans, credit cards, lines of credit, mortgages, etc.). Use these tools wisely and they can help build your financial future. Use them carelessly and your finances will reel from the blow.

If you're going to use credit of any kind, be sure that you understand exactly what you're getting into. Ask questions and educate yourself. Is the kind of credit that you're looking at the right tool for what you need to achieve? For instance, a charge card, with its high interest rate, probably isn't the best choice for making a major purchase if you'll be carrying a balance for a while.

The kind of credit tool you choose will depend on a number of factors, including:

• What you'll be using it for

• Interest rates

• Repayment terms

• Your ability to pay

Mortgages, Loans, and Credit Lines

As more and more financial institutions are entering the competition for your dollar, terms for mortgages, loans, and credit lines are becoming increasingly creative. You can pay monthly, bi-weekly, or weekly. You can pay down your principal by various amounts each year. You can have a fixed rate, or a variable rate. Penalties for early payout will also vary.

With such fierce competition for your business, it pays to shop around for a mortgage or a loan just as you would for any other major purchase. Investigating the various options will take time, but could ultimately save you a great deal of money (tens of thousands of dollars over the life of your mortgage). Translate that into an hourly rate and your time becomes very valuable indeed!

Student Loans

Students who go on to college or university often don't have the financial means to pay for their continuing education on their own. If family finances and part-time jobs don't cover all the costs associated with a higher education, loans are available to qualified students (including some who are attending school part-time) through the Canadian and provincial governments. An excellent one-stop source of information is available online at www.canlearn.ca, a Web site that provides everything you need to know to help plan and finance education and training (including information about universities, colleges, scholarships, and more). It also includes the National Student Loans Service Centre, which will help you apply for, maintain, or repay student loans.

Some financial institutions also offer student loans. These are not federally or provincially approved student loans, but simply a regular loan with the word "student" attached. Some institutions offer students a straight loan, while others offer a line of credit that allows students to access money as needed. Interest rates on these loan options are usually higher than the government rates.

Credit Cards

While we've already discussed the pitfalls of credit cards earlier in this book, you should also be aware of some of the proactive steps you can take to reduce the cost of using one.

- Read your agreement. You might be surprised to find out what your card is really costing you. Look at what your interest rate is (usually 15 to 20 per cent). Find out the policy on cash advances (most times you pay interest on these from the moment you take out the money until you've paid off the preceding balance plus the cash advance). Check to see if you're paying an annual fee. Read all the fine print, then decide if your card is worth keeping or if it's simply costing you too much.

- Credit cards often offer a low introductory rate in order to attract clients. Find out what your credit card company's introductory rate is, and call them. Tell them that, because you're a good customer, you think you should also be offered a lower rate (it may not be quite as low as the introductory offer, but you could still end up with a greatly reduced rate). If you carry a balance on another card, offer to transfer that balance to this card in exchange for the lower rate and an increased limit. If all else fails, tell them that you'll take your business elsewhere if they can't accommodate your request—and then be prepared to do so.

- Ride the wave! It's called "credit card surfing." By constantly seeking the lowest introductory rates on other cards and shifting your balances accordingly, you can in effect ride the interest wave. To make this work for you, be sure that you don't miss the opportunity to change cards before the introductory rate period is up (read the fine print!), and that the new card will accept the old balance transfer without a fee. A word of caution: Credit card hopping too often can actually damage your credit rating. It's best to stick with your choice of card for at least a year so that your history shows some stability.

SUCCESS TIP

If you take advantage of a low introductory rate on a credit card, make sure you keep your payments up to date. One late payment, and you can kiss the low rate goodbye.

- Know your billing cycle. To avoid interest charges, purchases made within your billing cycle (the date of the next cycle should be on your bill) must be paid by the next bill. If you wait until the next billing cycle to make a planned purchase (no impulses allowed!), you can extend your grace period (the period during which you don't pay interest) for the entire next billing cycle.

Example

Your credit card statement is dated the 14th of July and the payment is due August 4th (21 days later) By waiting until July 15th to make your purchase, the charge will appear on your next statement, e.g. August 14th, and payment will only be due on September 4th. By waiting one day, you extend your grace period by an additional 30 days!

• Limit the number of cards you carry. Too many sources of credit (even if you're not carrying a balance on your cards, they count as a source) can be hazardous to your financial health. Most of us need only one or two major cards, and we can probably do without store cards altogether. Fewer cards, less temptation, fewer payments, less interest...I'm sure you see the big picture.

CONSUMER BE WARY

The consumer-driven world that we live in is full of potential problems and pitfalls. Marketers are intent on selling you everything they can think of (most of which you'll never need), companies are constantly dreaming up new ways to serve you (for a price, of course), and scam artists are doing their level best to separate you from whatever dollars that you may have left over.

What's a poor consumer to do?

There's only one thing you can do, and that's refuse to *be* a poor consumer—in either the figurative or the literal sense. Take charge of your dollars, and refuse to give them away unless you're absolutely certain that it's for a worthy cause (either your own or someone else's). Don't be taken in by anyone or anything. Ask questions, educate yourself, stay informed, and always be skeptical. A smart consumer knows that if something looks too good to be true, it probably is.

Payday Loans/Cheque Cashing Services

Make no mistake, this is no "service" at all, but a very expensive form of temporary credit (think loan sharks). Payday loans and cheque cashing services are expensive; so expensive, in fact, that their charges border on (and in some cases, are) criminal. The fees and service charges attached to these loans count as interest in the eyes of the courts, and can range from 50 to over 1,000 per cent—

making some of them illegal under Canada's Criminal Code (because of court backlogs, however, cases are rarely prosecuted).

PAYDAY LOANS:

How They Really Work

Write a personal cheque for $115 to borrow $100 for 14 days. The check casher will hold the cheque up to 14 days until your next payday. At that time, depending on the particular plan, the cheque casher deposits the cheque, you redeem the cheque by paying $115 in cash, or you roll over the cheque by paying a fee to extend the loan for another 2 weeks. In this example, the cost of the initial loan is a $15 finance charge for 14 days or 391% APR.

Unfortunately, until these services are better regulated, it's very much a case of buyer beware. If you're using—or tempted to use—the service, don't. If money is short between paydays, go back to Chapter Three and try to find another way of surviving your budget shortfall.

White-Label or No-Name ATMs

They're springing up everywhere these days, making accessing cash easier than ever. But are they a good thing? Not really. White-label, or no-name, ATMs are independently operated by private businesses and carry hefty convenience fees. Use one and you not only pay your regular bank transaction fee plus the network access (Interac) fee, but an additional charge that could bring your total fee to $5.50 or more than 27 per cent in fees on a $20 withdrawal!

Instead of accessing your cash with one of these machines, use the "cash back" option when you make a purchase at most grocery stores, pharmacies, liquor stores, etc., for true, fee-free convenience.

Internet Shopping: The New Frontier in E-commerce

Rapidly becoming more acceptable, shopping online is without doubt fast, convenient, and efficient. It's a great way of comparing prices and specifications, and for locating that perfect gift or hard-to-find item. You can even get special discounts from some retailers if you purchase online.

Because of its easy access, however, the Internet also makes it easy to over-shop. When you remember that you're probably using credit for your purchases (most online retailers will accept payment only by credit card), you can see the danger involved. You also have to remember that in many cases you're paying in U.S. dollars, and that you'll have to pay shipping, handling, duty, and GST (this is charged at the border by Customs when an item enters Canada). You can bypass some of this additional expense by shopping at a Canadian site when available (e.g., Amazon.ca instead of Amazon.com).

There are also some unscrupulous sites out there that are more interested in getting your money than they are in delivering the promised goods, so you need to use some common sense in your online purchasing. These tips might help:

- Know who you're buying from. Looking like a legitimate business on the Web isn't difficult, so make sure that you check out any company you're not familiar with. Look for membership in the Better Business Bureau, evaluations of products in hard-copy magazines, and so on.

- Know what you're getting. A picture may be worth a thousand words, but it can also be very deceiving if it's the only thing you have to go by. If you're not sure about what you're ordering, call the company first—and while you're on the phone, ask about their return policy, too.

- Know what you're paying. If you buy from the U.S., you'll be paying in U.S. dollars. You'll also be paying duty and GST on the item when it comes through Customs. If you buy from within your home province, provincial sales tax applies. Shipping and handling almost always apply.

- Know what you're agreeing to. The provider agreement is posted for a reason—read it! If something is written there that you didn't know about, you can't claim ignorance if things go wrong. If you don't understand the company's policy, call and ask for clarification.

- Know you're secure. If you're giving out your credit card information online, make sure that it's being sent over a secure and protected Web site and server (most legitimate companies advertise this fact).

- Use your printer liberally. Print all contracts and receipts and keep them for your protection.

- And finally, guard your privacy. Just about every Web site out there wants your information, and you need to know why before you hand it out. Those elaborate privacy policies that many reputable sites have aren't always as complete as you might think, so once again, read the fine print!

Online Auctions

A big *buyer beware* on this topic. Online auctions seem like a great idea, but many an unwary purchaser has been burned. To minimize your own risk if you decide to participate in an online auction service, follow these tips:

- If you buy from a private individual, consumer protection laws don't apply. In other words, if you don't receive what you thought you paid for, you have no legal recourse. The auction site may have a resolution service for disputes, but this service is likely very limited. Read the disclaimer posted on the site for details.

- For the above reason, check out the seller as best you can before you bid. The site's feedback registry will tell you what other buyers thought of the seller's product, promptness, etc., but even that isn't foolproof. If you have any suspicions that a seller isn't being forthright, or if the seller has no history, consider passing on that particular item. If you decide to go ahead with your bid, get a description of the item in writing so that you at least have some basis for a complaint if the item doesn't live up to your expectations.

• Remember that purchases from the U.S. (or any other country), even if private, are still international purchases that are subject to shipping, currency exchange, duties, and taxes.

• If you're purchasing an item, confirm with the seller that it will insure the package if the item is lost or damaged in shipping.

• An online offer is a binding contract, so be selective and be prepared to win. This is especially true if you've put your bidding into the hands of the site's robot bidder: You may be shocked to find out that you now have to come up with the cash for that lava lamp that seemed like such a great buy at 3 a.m.

Scam Busting

The schemes are plentiful. Unfortunately, so are the people who buy into them. Every year, thousands of Canadians are burned by scams that grow ever more elaborate in order to outsmart the consumer and evade the law. Here are some of the more common ones that you need to be aware of:

• Advanced Fee Letter Fraud: These letters arrive in Canadian homes and businesses by fax, mail, and email (email is the preferred method), and concern a "request for urgent business transaction"—usually the transfer of millions of dollars. Stressing the importance of trust and honesty, the letter's writer, often claiming to be a doctor or a representative of a major corporation, asks the recipient to call for further information. When contact is established, the recipient will ask for an upfront processing fee, or for a meeting to discuss the transfer of funds.

- Prize Pitch: You're asked to purchase a product and pay in advance in order to claim a prize. Products range from coin collections to vacation packages, and are never what you're led to expect.

- Recovery Pitch: A follow-up to the prize pitch. If you buy into the first, you'll likely be called again, this time by someone promising to get your money back for you (for a small fee, of course). The person could even claim to be a law enforcement officer (if a legitimate police agency does seize money, you'll be advised but never asked for money).

- Advanced Fee Loans: A company advertises that they can guarantee you a loan regardless of your credit history...once more, for a fee. These ads generally appear in the classifieds.

- Travel: Shortly after filling out a ballot to win a vacation, you're contacted by someone offering you a "free" or "low-cost" vacation. They ask for your credit card number in order to hold the vacation for you, or for an advance fee.

SUCCESS TIP

Never give out your credit card information to a travel telemarketer.

If you do make this mistake, be aware that most companies have policies allowing you to cancel within 30 days.

- False Charities: If you've never heard of a charitable organization, be cautious about donating. A legitimate charity will be happy to send you information by mail or give you time to check them out.

- Pyramid Schemes: This type of fraud is based on recruiting investors who are then expected to recruit more investors, and so on. Emphasis is placed on recruiting rather than selling products or distributorships, until the recruit pool runs dry and the last investors (at the bottom of the pyramid) lose their money.

- 1-900 Scams: A variation on the prize pitch that encourages you to call a 1-900 number to find out how much money or what prize you've won. The prize is generally a couple of dollars, and each call you make to the number can cost you up to $35.

High-Pressure Sales Tactics

While they don't qualify as scams, high-pressure sales tactics can still relieve you of a big chunk of money and leave you holding something that you really don't want or need, and that often you can't even afford. Time-shares and vacuum cleaner sales are two that spring to mind.

A good rule to remember when you're facing pressure tactics from a polished salesperson is that you can always think it over and take the deal tomorrow if you still like it. If you're told that you have to act now, don't just walk away, *run*. I can guarantee you that kind of deal is absolutely not worth it.

Another tip is to have someone whose objectivity you trust along with you (not necessarily your spouse, who may be just as inclined to get caught up in the excitement of the moment as you are). It's harder for the salesperson to convince you to sign when he or she is facing two sets of questions.

The Consumer Protection Act of Ontario gives you a cooling off period for purchases over $50, but only under certain circumstances and *never for time-shares*:

- The goods must be delivered in the future.

- The contract is not made in the seller's place of business (if you're dealing with a door-to-door salesperson, that would be your home).

Other provinces have similar legislation. A list of the Provincial Consumer Protection Agencies is set out in Appendix "D".

CHAPTER SUMMARY

- Avoiding impulse purchases by devising ways to cool off before making a decision.

- Emergency purchases can often be delayed.

- Major purchases should be planned for to avoid hasty decisions.

- Planning a vacation is more than deciding when and where; consider all the expenses.

- Holiday shopping can easily get out of control. Start with a plan and a budget.

- Credit tools can both help and hinder your financial situation. Always know what you're getting into.

- Consumer pitfalls are everywhere, and awareness is key to making proper decisions.

CHAPTER SEVEN

Coping with the Unforeseen

How to Handle Dietary Setbacks

"A banker is a fellow who lends you his umbrella when the sun is shining and wants it back the minute it begins to rain."
—Mark Twain

Life, as we all know from experience, can be unpredictable. Sometimes, despite our best efforts and intentions, we're caught off guard by the unexpected. While the scenarios that we look at in this chapter (job loss, marital breakdown, incapacitation, death) are considerably more serious than a simple dietary falling-off-the-wagon, the remedy is pretty much the same: You still have to pick yourself up, dust yourself off, and get back on track.

If you've had the chance to put your financial affairs in order and get yourself started on the road to future success (including following the planning tips you will find in Chapter Ten), then chances are that you'll be in a fairly good position to weather a financial diet setback.

But what if you've only just started on your debt reduction, and you haven't yet taken care of all the details? What if life hits you with a major disaster at a time when you are least prepared to handle it?

My best advice is *don't panic*. You aren't the first person to be caught unaware, and you won't be the last. No matter what your financial setback, there are steps that you can take—even after the fact—to minimize the damage and put you back on the path to financial health as quickly as possible.

JOB LOSS

If you have advance warning or suspect that you're going to lose your job (perhaps due to company downsizing), you should immediately develop a contingency plan. Meet with your soon-to-be-former employer to discuss your severance package, and don't be afraid to negotiate for more than what they're offering. If you feel uncomfortable negotiating, hire a lawyer who specializes in employment law.

Think of your severance pay as "bridge" money. Even if it is a large sum, remember that it has to tide you over until you find a new job, so don't be tempted to give in to the impulse to spend it on something like a family vacation or a new car. If you receive a particularly large lump sum, consider the possible tax consequences. If you can, you might want to top up your RRSP with some of this money in order to avoid paying income tax on it at your top marginal rate. A professional tax consultant can help you make necessary decisions.

The next step in your contingency plan is to set up a revised budget for your family. This will let you prioritize your spending and ensure that you'll be able to cover all of your expected costs while you're looking for new employment. Look at your current debt load to see if you can reduce it before your employment actually ends. If consolidating your debts will help, the time to apply for a consolidation loan or a new or increased line of credit is now, while you're still employed (and creditworthy in the eyes of a financial institution).

If you're let go or laid off without warning, and without a severance package, you *must* acknowledge and deal with the emotional aspects of job loss in order to effectively cope with the financial implications. Talk openly with your spouse/partner, and inform your children early on (in an age-appropriate manner); you're going to need their support in order to keep the family unit functioning smoothly in the face of sometimes-major changes. You'll also find that coping with budget cutbacks is a lot easier with your family's cooperation and understanding.

SUCCESS TIP

In an extreme cash crunch, you may have to prioritize your bills. Top priority should go to these essentials:

- Food and shelter (mortgage or rent)
- Utilities, phone, transportation, and insurance
- Secured debts (if you default on your car loan, you could find yourself suddenly without wheels)

Avoid letting pride get in your way. Remember that your primary concern at the moment is to keep your and your family's head above water. Don't panic. Be objective, stay calm, and be realistic.

First, apply immediately for unemployment benefits, which could take several weeks to kick in, depending on your circumstances. Then, take a critical look at your situation, decide what the worst-case scenario would really be, and prepare—at least mentally—to face that scenario. Even if you never need to use your worst-case contingency plan, you'll rest easier just knowing that you have one.

If you're not going to be able to meet all of your existing payments, let your creditors know *before* those payments are due. Explain your financial situation and let them know how long you expect the disruption to last, and how it will affect them. Most creditors, if they know that you're dealing with them in good faith, will try to arrange a lower payment plan with you, or even agree to suspend your payments altogether for a month or two. Just remember that once you reach an agreement with a creditor, you must be meticulous about following through on it. If you're unable to do so, keep the creditor apprised of your situation.

> **SUCCESS TIP**
>
> If you do find yourself in a job-loss or other "disaster" situation, remember that a credit counsellor (Chapter Two) can help put you back on financial track.

The temptation to use credit cards to see you through your financial crisis will be strong. Don't give in. With no way to pay down your charges or interest, you'll only be digging yourself into a deeper and deeper debt hole. Instead, find ways to cut expenses (cancel cable, give up your cell phone, suspend your gym membership) or to increase your income (sell the family's second vehicle, rent out a room in your home, have a non-working spouse find part-time employment). A review of Chapter Three will help you with a budget restructure.

Another temptation to avoid, wherever possible, is using your retirement nest egg. Cashing in an RRSP might seem like a good way to meet expenses during a job-loss crisis, but because of its immediate—and negative—tax implications, it should be a last resort.

If you've exhausted your unemployment benefits and/or severance package and still haven't found a new job, you may have to swallow your pride once again. Any job, whether you're overqualified for it or not, that can help you meet your expenses is infinitely preferable to going further into debt.

SEPARATION AND DIVORCE

If you and your spouse are facing the possibility of a marital breakdown, you should consult with an experienced family lawyer before you take any other steps—and, if possible, even before you separate. Family law is complex and varies from province to province. A lawyer who specializes in this area will be able to tell you how the law applies to your specific situation, and advise you on your best course of action. A family lawyer will cost you more than a general practice lawyer might, but it will definitely be worth the expense.

You can reduce your legal costs by doing some of the footwork yourself, such as gathering information your lawyer will need, including financial statements, tax returns, lists of assets and debts, and copies of pension plans, wills, trusts, and insurance policies.

Reducing Legal Costs in Divorce

- Ask your lawyer to assign routine tasks to junior and support staff (who charge a much lower hourly rate).

- Keep it short! Your lawyer will probably charge you for most conversations, including ones over the phone, so be prepared. Have your questions and information written down, and don't treat the conversation as a support/counselling session.

- Find out if mediation, which is cheaper than a court proceeding, is an option.

- Make sure that you get a written contract with your lawyer that sets out his/her hourly rate.

- Ask for itemized invoices, and don't be afraid to question charges that you don't understand (or that you feel are out of line).

No matter how amicable your breakup appears to be, you should take certain steps to protect yourself in the event that things turn ugly. Don't rely on joint accounts that you share with your spouse, who could close or empty them. Instead, open your own account, and begin depositing your income to that. Make an inventory of assets, including possessions and investments, and specify which of them are joint and which are individual. Get copies of all of your loan and mortgage documents, and avoid incurring any more debt. If you have joint credit cards, you may want to cancel them (remember, in writing) to prevent additional charges being made, but you'll have to pay out any balance owing first.

If you've never established your own credit rating, now is a very good time to do so (assuming that you're employed). See Chapter Four for ways to do this.

If you and/or your kids rely on your spouse's health insurance or dental coverage, make sure that your checkups and any necessary procedures are up-to-date. Also think about making repairs to your house and vehicle, updating your children's wardrobes, and dealing with other family expenses while joint funds are still available (rather than having to argue with your spouse later about who should be responsible).

Even if your separation and divorce seem to be going smoothly, be prepared for the worst—especially if you're a woman—because the sad fact is that you will often suffer financially after separation. While courts can and do order spousal and child support, most such payments are in arrears. If you find yourself in a position where support has been ordered, but isn't being paid, ask your lawyer about getting government intervention. Most provincial governments have agencies that are responsible for ensuring that spousal and child support orders are honoured.

Faced with a "Deadbeat"?

If your spouse isn't making the ordered support payments, you should know these facts:

- Even if you enlist the aid of your provincial government agency, the backlog is usually huge, and getting actual payment will take a while.

- Some provinces (such as Ontario) require that an employer deduct support payments from wages. However, a determined deadbeat may try to avoid this by moving.

- It is still difficult to enforce court orders between provinces, or out of country, but not always impossible. Make sure your lawyer checks all possibilities.

- Support payments generally survive bankruptcy.

The division of family property is governed by provincial law and therefore varies widely, so be sure to ask your lawyer's advice. However, in general, you should be aware of the following:

1. *The Family Home*
   - Both you and your spouse usually have an equal right to this asset. If one chooses to stay in the home, he/she will have to pay half the value to the other.

   - If having one spouse buy out the other is not an option, an alternative is to swap assets (e.g., one spouse may transfer an RRSP to the other in exchange for his/her interest in the property. This is a very complicated legal area, so get professional help.)

   - The last option would be to sell the home and divide the net proceeds between the two parties.

2. *Pension Funds*
   - Next to the family home, a pension is often the second most valuable marital asset. It's also one of the most contentious issues, requiring complex negotiations (essentially, you're trying to put a present value on an asset that won't be paid until much later, and one that relies on investment market fluctuations). Be prepared to pay your advisor to have this done.

   - CPP and QPP benefits accrued during the marriage can be split up after the divorce (pension credits can be transferred); you can do this without your lawyer's help by filling in the necessary forms, but you should still discuss the matter with your lawyer as the amounts will affect your overall negotiation strategy in the divorce settlement.

3. *Other Assets*
   - Don't forget about other assets such as cars, boats, cottages, collections, heirlooms, business assets, investments, etc. Even items such as AIR MILES are sometimes viewed as assets.

Post-divorce, you may find that child support payments cover true essentials, but not other "necessities" that most kids will need. You can save yourself a lot of grief and a costly legal battle over child support amounts if you can reach an agreement with your partner about sharing major expenses, such as dental bills, music/dance lessons, and summer camp costs.

If you decide to remarry, remember that your earlier obligations take priority! You cannot decide that your new family is more important that your first one, and you can't arbitrarily reduce support payments. If you're the one receiving support, know that remarrying or even living with someone can trigger an application for a reduction in child or spousal support. Discuss the implications with your new partner and your lawyer.

SUCCESS TIP

Planning a second family? Make sure you make financial plans, too!

- Increase your emergency funds to cover support payments plus new-family expenses.
- Increase your life insurance coverage.
- Start education savings for the expected additions.
- Revise your will to reflect your changed situation.

INCAPACITATION

If you are disabled or ill (and unable to work) for an extended time, you could face a serious decline in your living standards—or even a descent into poverty—because of your sudden loss of income. The only real way to handle this particular diet disaster is to plan for it through disability insurance. Then, if you do become disabled, apply for your benefits as soon as possible. Don't wait until you've used up your other resources such as your savings. It can take time for your benefits to begin rolling in, and you'll have enough to worry about (like recuperating) without adding financial stress to the picture.

If you aren't sure about the details of your disability policy, don't hesitate to get professional help. Remember that insurance companies make their money from collecting premiums, not from paying out benefits, so they're not likely to go out of their way to make things easy for you.

If your disability results from an injury on the job, you may be eligible for Workers' Compensation, but don't think that you can rely on this program to help you meet your obligations. First of all, these provincial programs generally provide only subsistence payments: The list of potential benefits may look extensive—in Ontario, these benefits include Loss of Earnings, Non-Economic Loss, Loss of Retirement Income, Health Care Benefits, Occupational Disease and Survivor Benefits, and Benefits for Seriously Injured Workers—but in reality, coverage is basic and unlikely to cover what you need it to.

Second, there are tough restrictions on eligibility, along with regular reviews. You'll have to put in a lot of time and energy just to get the benefits. For your own peace of mind, and your family's, make sure that you have disability coverage through insurance.

DEATH AND INTESTACY

I cannot overstress the importance of having a will. To die intestate—without a will—creates a tremendous amount of hardship and strain for your family at a time when they are least able to cope. That said, however, the reality is that some people won't, unfortunately, take this advice. What then?

Any grief counsellor will suggest that you not do anything "drastic," such as selling your home, within the first year of your spouse's death, because you're most likely not thinking clearly. This is excellent advice—most of the time. If your spouse has died without a will, leaving you in a financial crisis, you may not have the luxury of time. The following suggestions are based on that premise.

If you are joint tenants on your home, the home will automatically vest in you (except in Quebec: there, the deceased's portion is frozen until the courts determine how the estate will be dealt with). If you have a mortgage on the house, find out if there is any mortgage life insurance. If there is, the house will be paid off and you will own it free and clear.

With this kind of equity in your home, you have three choices: One, you can keep the house if you think you'll have enough money from other assets to cover your living expenses; two, you can sell the house and use part of the equity to purchase something smaller, and the other part to cover your living expenses; or three, if you have a shortfall in your living expenses, you can remortgage the house using a line of credit that you can draw on as needed.

As the survivor, you will also automatically have the right to any jointly held bank accounts. The exception to this is once again in Quebec: Any joint bank accounts in Quebec banks are frozen until the disposal of the estate is determined.

If the deceased spouse owned stocks or other investments and you are not the named beneficiary, you will have to apply to the court to be appointed as the estate administrator. This will enable you to function much the same as an executor under a will. You may, however, have to post a bond—for up to twice the value of the estate—with the court to ensure that you comply with the court's requirements.

A surviving spouse may also be entitled to other benefits. A death benefit of approximately $2,500 is offered by government of Canada (you'll need to apply for this), and you can also apply to see if you are entitled to survivor's benefits for yourself and your children. Check with your deceased spouse's workplace as well to see if there are any death benefits available from the employer.

If your spouse has died intestate, you could be faced with a considerable cash crunch while (and even after) you sort out the estate, assets, and other details. If this is the case, you'll need to cut your expenses—and increase your income—as soon as possible. Here are some considerations:

• Liquidate as many assets as you can. Did your spouse own any collections that can be sold? What about a second vehicle that's no longer in use?

• Downsize your accommodations. If you can sell the house, do so, then look for something smaller and more affordable, or even rent for a while until you're back on your feet.

• Move in with family. If things are really tight, think about moving in with a willing relative or friend for a short time.

• Rent out a room. If you're determined to hold onto your house, but need help meeting the expenses, take in a student or boarder.

• If you're not already employed, find a job. If you've been staying at home to look after kids or pursue a small home-based business up until now, your new reality may not allow for you to continue doing so.

Intestacy laws vary from province to province. (See Appendix "E" for a summary of the intestacy laws in your province.) If you should happen to be caught in the very difficult and unfortunate position of having to deal with an estate where there is no will, my best advice is to seek the assistance of a wills and estates lawyer who will advise you on dealing with the necessary court applications.

And if you happen to be reading this and still don't have your own will in place, remember that the above intestacy scenario is not only unfortunate, it is entirely preventable. Do your loved ones a favour and get a will (and a power of attorney while you're at it).

DEBTS OWED TO YOU

Another financial diet setback that you could face is a case where you're depending on money that is owed to you, but the person or company is refusing to pay. If you find yourself in this situation, you may need to take the matter to small claims court—the simplest and most effective method of recovering money for things like overdue payments and unpaid contracts.

To be tried in most provincial small claims courts, a claim must be for:

- Money that is owed to you (a loan that hasn't been repaid, an NSF cheque, etc.), *or*

- Damages that were caused by another person's actions (property damage caused by another person's negligence, for instance), *or*

- The return of personal property held by another person, *or*

- (In Ontario) property damage under the *Parental Responsibility Act 2000*.

Claim limits vary from province to province, but court procedures are similar across the country:

- You pay a filing fee (usually less than $100) to start your claim.

- You have to file your claim in the area where it originated, or where the defendant (the person you're suing) lives or does business.

- You have to "serve," or formally deliver, your claim to the defendant (either personally, through a process server, or by other means as prescribed by law).

- If you win and the defendant still doesn't pay you, you can have the judgment enforced through the seizure and sale of assets, garnishment of wages, and other methods.

SUCCESS TIP

If you decide to do it yourself, pick up a guide to trying a small claims action. It may be the best investment you make!

If you do take a claim to court, the court will encourage you to "settle," or come to an agreement with the defendant; it may even require a settlement conference before it tries the case. If you *can* settle, it will save you a costly trial (even if you decide to represent yourself, remember that you'll still be losing time—and wages— while you're in court).

Other things you should know about small claims:

- In your claim, you can ask for interest on the money that is owed to you. The court usually applies a statutory interest rate, but you can claim more if your contract or invoice specifies a higher rate.

- If you win, and the defendant doesn't pay you immediately, you can also claim post-judgment interest.

- If your claim is more than the court's limit, you can forego the extra and just ask for the maximum (make it clear in your claim that you're doing this). You cannot, however, divide your claim into two actions in an attempt to bypass the court's limit.

- If you're successful in your claim, you can ask for costs to cover things like lost wages, transportation, filing fees, claim-service fees, photocopies, and faxes, etc.

A FINAL WORD

When it comes to dealing with financial disasters, the old adage "an ounce of prevention is worth a pound of cure" could not be any truer. By taking the time and making the effort now to ensure that your finances are in order, you can save yourself and your family countless hours of stress and heartache.

Review your insurance policies. Get disability insurance. Have a will and power of attorney drawn up. Think about worst-case scenarios, plan how you'll deal with them, and then file your plans away in your new, well-organized financial files and relax, knowing that you and your family are covered in the event of financial setbacks.

Disasters happen. How we choose to deal with them is entirely up to us.

CHAPTER SUMMARY

- Job loss can be a disaster if you don't prepare for, or take the necessary steps after, the loss.

- Separation and divorce can, and often do, turn messy. Take the time to separate your financial assets, and speak to a lawyer to protect you and your family.

- Prepare for incapacitation by taking out disability insurance.

- Some of the pressures of your death and intestacy can be avoided.

- Debts owed to you can be obtained through legal proceedings.

Taxes

Avoiding Income Indigestion

"The hardest thing in the world to understand is the income tax."
—Albert Einstein

Taxes. People groan at the very mention of the word, and who can blame them? The thought of paying up to 50 per cent or more of our hard-earned income every year to a system that most of us don't even really understand...well, who among us enjoys that task? But detest them as we might, taxes are very much an unavoidable part of our lives and our finances.

What amazes me is the number of people who know that income tax is inevitable, and yet still try to evade the issue by either filing late, or by not even filing at all! In my opinion, this is sheer madness because not only will these people eventually get caught (and potentially prosecuted), they'll also owe a lot more money than they would have if they'd just filed and paid on time. If you happen to be one of the vegetable avoiders, then you need to pay close attention to these words:

TAXES ARE YOUR RESPONSIBILITY!

There's no point to ignoring them; you can't hide from them or get out of them; we all have to pay them; and no, you don't have a choice in the matter. Income tax is a simple fact of life—and it's the law. Period. End of discussion.

However, if you're smart, you also *plan* for them.

FILING YOUR RETURN

Personal income tax returns for any given year are due by April 30 of the following year. In other words, your tax return for 2003 will be due by April 30, 2004. If you know—or suspect—that you may owe taxes at that time, *plan* for it. Start setting aside a little each month so that you don't face (or try to avoid) a huge bill and major indigestion come tax time.

For example, if a person owes $1,800 in outstanding taxes and files one week late, they would owe $2.42 in interest plus $90 in penalty charges.

Who Has to File?

You're required to file an income tax return if:

- You've received a notice from Canada Customs and Revenue Agency (CCRA) to file.

- You earned more than $3,500 in a year (over that amount, you also have to pay CPP).

- You owe more tax than was deducted from your pay.

- You have to repay part (or all) of your employment insurance or old age benefits because your income exceeded allowable limits.

- You haven't repaid what you owe under the Home Buyers' Plan.

- You want to claim for, and are eligible for, tax credits (GST, Child Tax Benefits, etc.).

- You're a student with tuition or education amounts that have to be carried forward.

- Your excess charitable donations have to be carried forward (you can do this for up to five years).

- You have capital gains, even if they're offset by capital losses or exemptions (losses can be carried forward indefinitely).

If you're the sole owner of, or a partner in, an unincorporated business, your return isn't due until June 15 of the following year. Your spouse can also file by this date (meaning that both your tax returns for 2003 will be due by June 15, 2004). However, your actual taxes are still due by the April 30 deadline, so even if you don't file until the 15th of June, you'll still need to pay in April, or else face interest charges (from the April 30 due date until you file and pay in June) on the amount you owe.

What You May Not Know—But Need To!

- If you are self-employed and owe $2,000 or more in the prior or current taxation year, you must make instalments! In other words, if you owed $3,000 last year, or think that you will this year, you need to prepay your income taxes.

- Tax instalments are due on March 15, June 15, September 15, and December 15 of the current year (i.e., in 2004 for the 2004 taxation year).

- If your instalments aren't made on time, a penalty is applied to any outstanding instalment amount.

Penalties and Interest

Canada Customs and Revenue Agency, or CCRA (still known to many Canadians as Revenue Canada), exists to collect taxes from you—not to cater to the irregularities in your personal schedule, your financial troubles, or your lack of foresight. If you file your return after the due date, CCRA will charge a five per cent penalty on any amount that you owe, in addition to any interest! So if you owe $3,500 in outstanding income tax and you're a month late, you'll pay $20.42 interest (calculated at the current seven per cent) plus $175 in penalty charges (calculated at the current five per cent). The interest charge compounds and applies to any outstanding balance owed to

CCRA; it continues to apply until the balance is paid off. The penalty, on the other hand, is a one-time charge levied for a late return—and if your return is more than one month overdue, you're charged an *additional* one per cent for every month you're late (to a maximum of 12 months). You can see now why you should plan to file on time.

SUCCESS TIP

Always file your return on time.

Even if you can't pay what you owe, you must still file your return. You'll need to pay interest on any outstanding balance, but filing on time means that you avoid any additional penalties (and possible interruption of government benefits such as Old Age Security and Canada Pension). Then, when you receive your notice of assessment from CCRA, you can make payment arrangements by contacting a tax services office.

Because interest is charged at a compounded daily rate, the cost of "borrowing" from CCRA (which is essentially what you're doing by paying instalments or paying late) can be very expensive. A better route might be to arrange a loan to pay off the full amount now. You'll still be making payments, of course, but at a much lower overall interest rate.

If you prefer to make instalments to CCRA in spite of the higher interest, try to send a series of postdated cheques for the length of time you need to pay your taxes in full. This will help to ensure that you stick with a payment plan, and that you don't find yourself still owing this year's taxes when next year's become due.

Late Filing Need-to-Knows

Even though CCRA isn't there to make your tax-life comfortable for you, neither is it completely unreasonable. If you've missed a tax-filing deadline because of circumstances beyond your control, you may be able to have penalty and interest charges waived. Ask

CCRA for their information circular 92-2, *Guidelines for the Cancellation and Waiver of Interest and Penalties*, or check their Web site, www.ccra-adrc.gc.ca, for more information.

The most critical thing to remember is that no matter how late you do so, you must file. Beyond penalties and interest for late filing, you run a very real risk of prosecution for tax evasion if you don't file at all. Under CCRA's fairness initiative, you may be able to avoid prosecution and have penalties waived through the Voluntary Disclosures Program if your disclosure:

• Is voluntary

• Is complete

• Involves a penalty

• Involves a disclosure at least one year overdue

You'll still have to pay your taxes owed.

More information on this program is available on CCRA's Web site, www.ccra-adrc.gc.ca, or you can call CCRA on a hypothetical basis (naming no names) to discuss the situation.

Repeat Offenders Beware!

If you've already been charged a late-filing penalty in the last three years, your penalty for filing late again could be even higher than five per cent!

Notice of Assessment

Once you've filed your income tax return, CCRA will review it and, if everything is in order, send you a Notice of Assessment. The notice will tell you if you've filed correctly, and will show any adjustments that have been made to your return. It will also indicate how much room you have available for your next year's RRSP contributions, so be sure to keep the notice for your records.

The Notice of Assessment is not binding. CCRA can reassess you at any time within three years of mailing the original notice. Your time for reviewing your numbers is somewhat less than that: If you discover that you've overpaid your taxes, you have 90 days from the notice's mailing date to file a Notice of Objection, or one year from the due date of that particular return, whichever is later.

TAX-SAVING STRATEGIES

Just as vegetables can be made more palatable if they're masked in a casserole, taxes can be easier on the digestion if you know you're at least taking advantage of all the possible deductions and strategies. To do this, step beyond the actual filing and payment to planning. Every dollar that you're able to deduct from your return decreases your taxable income by that same dollar, translating into savings at your marginal rate (the marginal rate is the top limit for taxing your income; in most provinces, it's about 50 per cent of your income).

Income tax laws become more complex every year (in spite of CCRA's "simplification" strategies), so if you're not aware of, or willing to learn about, the various strategies and deductions, it might be worth your while to have your return worked out by a professional.

Deductions

If you decide you're up to taking on the tax challenge yourself, make sure you take all available deductions. As necessary as taxes are to our country's structure, you'd much rather have the extra dollars in your pocket instead of the government's. So go ahead and take advantage of what's available to you:

• RRSP contributions—the biggest deductions you can get. You can contribute up to 18 per cent of your income in a year, and the income in your RRSP won't be taxed until you begin withdrawing the money after you retire (by which time, your income will most likely be lower, so you'll actually pay less tax).

- If your spouse's income is lower than your own, you can contribute to his or her RRSP (a spousal RRSP) from your own income (up to your spouse or common-law partner's RRSP limit) and claim the deductions on your own tax return.

Separated or Divorced?

You may be able to claim some of your legal fees as a deduction.

While you cannot deduct fees for obtaining a lump sum or for obtaining spousal support, you can deduct fees for *enforcing* spousal support, and for obtaining and enforcing child support.

Ask your lawyer to itemize the bill for their services so that you can claim the appropriate amounts.

- Commissioned salesperson? Look for deductions on expenses that aren't reimbursed by your employer. Consider leasing your cellphone, computer, and fax machine instead of buying them. You can't claim capital cost allowance on these items if you're on commission.

- Claim medical expenses on the return of the spouse who has the lowest income.

- If you have student loans, you can carry the interest forward for up to five years, letting you claim the interest when your income is higher and you need the deductions more.

Commonly Missed Deductions

Are you claiming all that you can? Here are some deductions that many people forget/don't know about:

- Moving expenses if you move at least 40 km closer to your new place of work or educational institution than your previous home was

- Child-care expenses (if you're working or attending school) including day care, nursery, babysitting, camp, and boarding school lodging
- Safety deposit box fees
- Charitable donations
- Political contributions
- Medical expenses
- Interest on debts for expenses used to earn income (check with a tax professional because this is tricky)
- Any foreign taxes that you pay

Tax Credits

There's more than one casserole recipe for vegetables, and more than one method of reducing your taxes. As well as deductions, be aware of tax credits for which you may be eligible—these are the exemptions that reduce your taxes after you've calculated what you owe, and are especially important for low-income earners. The basic personal exemption (in 2002, $7,634) can be claimed for anyone who files a return, including children.

Should Your Child File a Tax Return?

The main benefit of having children file a tax return is to maximize their lifetime RRSP contribution limit.

Regardless of whether their total income is below the tax threshold, they can begin to create RRSP contribution room as soon as they file their first return (they don't need to contribute immediately).

RRSP contribution room is generated only by income from work, and not from income earned from interest, dividends, capital gains, scholarships, or bursaries.

In addition to the basic personal exemption, you can also claim charitable donations as a tax credit—16 per cent of the first $200 in donations, and 29 per cent of anything over that. If you haven't claimed your charitable donations in past years, you may be able to do so now (certain conditions may apply, so check with CCRA before you claim). If you're married, make sure that all of your donations are deducted from only one of your returns—remember, you're aiming to be in the 29 per cent tax-credit bracket. Even if the receipts are in your name, they can still be claimed on your spouse's return.

Did You Know?

Under the Income Tax Act, same-sex couples are now treated as spouses. They can claim all spousal deductions and credits, and can contribute to spousal RRSPs under the same rules that used to apply only to opposite-sex married and common-law couples.

If your spouse or common-law partner doesn't need all of his or her tax credits in order to reduce taxable income to zero, you can claim the leftover portion on your return.

Tuition fees, education credits, pension credits, disability credits, and age credits can all be transferred. Unused tuition and education tax credits can also be transferred to a supporting parent or grandparent.

SUCCESS TIP

For maximum tax advantages when filing spousal returns, higher-income earners should use the deductions, and lower-income earners should use the tax credits.

Excluded Benefits

Another way to save on your taxes is through excluded benefits. CCRA doesn't consider all income taxable, including some employee benefits, or "perks." If you're able to negotiate with your employer, it might be in your best interests to take such a perk instead of an increase in salary. Your employer won't have to make payroll deductions on these perks, so the arrangement is to their benefit, too. A word of caution, though, CCRA's list of reportable benefits is inconsistent at best, so be sure to check with a tax professional before you go this route.

Tax Planning for the Investor

For those of you who want to do more than just earn income and pay taxes, there are several tax tips that pertain to investing:

• Make sure you realize capital losses in order to set off capital gains.

• If you have kids, think about setting up a Registered Education Savings Plan (RESP). The contributions aren't deductible, but the investment earnings aren't taxed until they're withdrawn by your child for post-secondary education (who will most likely be in a lower tax bracket at the time).

RRSP-Specific Strategies

• Wherever possible, maximize your RRSP contributions, and don't wait until the deadline to do so. Rather than trying to scrape together the funds at the last minute (remember, you're planning here!), think about setting up an automatic withdrawal from your account (see Chapter Ten for more RRSP investment strategies).

• If you prefer to make a lump-sum RRSP contribution, make it as early in the taxation year as you can so that you can begin tax-free compounding as soon as possible.

- If you're turning 69 years old, you can make one final RRSP contribution that year before you convert your RRSP to an RRIF.
- Limit overcontributions to $2,000. Anything more than that at the end of any month is subject to a one per cent penalty.
- If your taxable income is low, carry forward your contribution and claim the deduction in a future, higher-income year.
- If you need to withdraw funds from an RRSP before you retire, limit the withdrawal to $5,000 or less per withdrawal in order to minimize with-holding tax (currently 10 per cent).

- If you make charitable donations, consider contributing publicly traded securities instead of cash...you can save on capital gains.

- If you borrow for investment purposes, the interest you pay on the debt is tax-deductible. If you're using a comingled cash account, you need to demonstrate that the aggregate eligible expenditures exceed the amount of borrowed money deposited to that account.

SUCCESS TIP

Minimize your non-deductible interest expenses: Pay down personal debts before you pay your investment-related ones!

- If you have joint investments with your spouse, the investment income is allotted between both of you based on your individual contributions to the investment.

- Choose wisely—not all investments carry the same tax benefits. Dividends, after the dividend tax credit, might yield a better return than fully taxable interest.

Tips for the Self-Employed

If you're a small business owner or self-employed, your business expenses are deductible. These expenses include interest on debts used to generate income (business loans), and health and dental insurance premiums. Also, if you start out operating at a loss, that loss can be carried forward for a number of years until you become profitable, at which time your income can be offset by your losses.

SUCCESS TIP

If you purchase a vehicle for work purposes, do so before the end of one tax year instead of at the beginning of the next. You'll accelerate the capital cost allowance claim by one year.

Another way to generate tax savings is to hire your spouse or child(ren). Get professional advice because you need to do this for a fair wage, for real work, and there are special considerations regarding the payment of minor children. The chief benefit to this arrangement is the increase in your spouse or child's taxable income and therefore their room for RRSP contributions. A bonus: Employment Insurance isn't generally required for "non-arm's length" employees such as family members. A drawback: Other payroll taxes, such as CPP, will be assessed and based on your actual employees, whether they are relatives or not.

Tips for Spouses

For most people, there are already many benefits to being married, but it's always nice to find an additional bonus to the state of matrimony. Income tax can actually provide just such a bonus for astute married planners who are able to shift income from the higher-tax bracket spouse to the lower one.

Income splitting, as it's called, is an effective way to lower your family's overall tax burden and increase its net worth. Because our taxation system is based on tax brackets (the more you earn, the more you pay), if you can redirect part of your income (assuming you're the one in the higher bracket) to your spouse, you can reap significant tax savings—$2,500 on a shift of $10,000 from a spouse in a 50 per cent bracket to one in a 25 per cent bracket.

Of course, it's not quite as simple as just assigning part of your income to your spouse on his or her tax return. As with every other tax matter, there are rules—attribution rules, to be exact. You'll have to be sure you learn those, and follow them closely, if you want to take advantage of income splitting the right way. The major rules involve gifts or loans to your spouse and/or adult children.

If you give money, property, or investments to your spouse, CCRA still attributes any profits or losses to you. The way around this is to sell the assets to your spouse at fair market value, or to lend the money or assets and charge interest.

In the case of an adult child (over 18), the rule of attribution doesn't apply to a gift of money or assets; any capital gains or losses affect the adult child's income, not yours. Attribution rules apply, however, if you made the loan in order to reduce your own taxes, or if your child invests the borrowed money so that he or she pays minimum tax on any interest received.

If you're interested in taking the income-splitting route, be sure you get your information straight. Call CCRA to find out what's allowed, or pay a professional to walk you through the procedures and answer your questions.

BEYOND PAYING: OTHER TAX RESPONSIBILITIES

Nothing tax-related is ever simple, but a little advance thinking and some organization—starting with your paperwork—can go a long way towards making it less difficult.

CCRA is not responsible for maintaining your records for you. *You* are. So do yourself a favour, and keep copies of all the T-slips, receipts, accounting records, and any documents you need to support your income tax returns. Remember that CCRA can ask to review your records at any time, for the current tax year and *up to seven previous years*. If you don't have the supporting documentation, CCRA has the right to arbitrarily reassess your income, and you could end up paying additional taxes plus penalties and interest (resulting in more indigestion!).

Papers to Keep

- T-slips
- RRSP contribution slips
- Medical receipts
- Charitable donation receipts
- Receipts and documents for self-employed income and expenses

---

Accountability

If there is a discrepancy between your T4 slip and the pay stubs you've received throughout the year, it's *your* responsibility to know about it and make sure it's corrected. CCRA assesses penalties for failing to report income, and it holds *you* responsible, not your employer. So keep those pay stubs, and compare them to your T4 when you receive it.

You are also responsible for accurate reporting of your investment income. When you receive your T3, T5, and other investment slips, check to see that the income and deduction amounts are reasonable, and keep those slips available for CCRA's review if necessary.

As for the returns themselves, no matter who does your return for you (spouse, bookkeeper, accountant, or tax professional), the responsibility for the accuracy—and for the timely filing—again belongs to you. You can't blame late filing, non-filing, or incomplete filing on anyone else, nor is anyone else liable for inaccurate information on your return. So take the time to review your return, ask questions about things that you don't understand, and if you're not satisfied, get another opinion from a tax professional.

CHANGES TO ALREADY-FILED RETURNS

If you discover that you've made an error on a previous year's return, you can make an online or mail request for a change or review.

To request a change by mail, send a completed form T1-ADJ (T1 Adjustment Request), or a *signed* letter that gives the details of your request, the year(s) of the return(s) you want changed, your social insurance number, your address, and your daytime phone number. Include with the letter any supporting documents for the changes, and (if you haven't sent them before) supporting documents for your original claim. You can request a refund for years as far back as 1985; adjustments usually take eight weeks to complete.

You can also ask for a change or review related to child and family benefits, or payments and interest, by contacting CCRA.

SUCCESS TIP

If you're expecting a refund from CCRA, wait to receive it before you spend it! You could be in for a nasty surprise if adjustments are made.

NETFILE AND OTHER CCRA SERVICES

If you haven't already tried NETFILE, or filing your tax return online, you might want to at least think about doing so.

In 2002, approximately 40 per cent of Canadians filed via the Internet, with benefits such as faster assessments, faster processing of refunds, and not-to-be-shrugged-off simple convenience. No more frantic, last-minute searches for stamps or near-midnight runs to the mailbox...just point, click, and done.

The NETFILE service continues to improve, too. CCRA is in the process of setting up an individual-accounts page called "My Account" for each of Canada's income-tax filers. Password protected and showing six years' worth of income tax assessments (including RRSP contribution room), the page will have calculators for GST rebates, child tax credits, and other benefits. The page will also allow online changes or adjustments to previous tax returns.

When NETFILE Is NOT an Option

NETFILE, while a convenient option for most Canadians, is not available to everyone. You cannot NETFILE your return if:

- This is your first tax return.

- You're correcting a mistake for this or a previous year.

- You're in bankruptcy.

- You're filing for your spouse (each return has to be sent in a separate file, with a separate access code).

- You're claiming a disability for the first time (for yourself or a dependant), or transferring a disability claim from your spouse to yourself.

- You're changing personal information, such as your name or address.

- You're requesting a re-deposit of funds.

And if you're wondering how the tax system maintains its integrity if people aren't required to send in their T4s or other documents, remember that this is the age of technology. CCRA can cross-check filers' information with employers and financial institutions at will.

Phone Filing

A new project begun in Atlantic Canada, Quebec, Saskatchewan, and Alberta in 2003 makes filing even easier for low-income seniors, who can file by phone without having to verify income figures.

During the phone-file, a person answers *yes* or *no* to a series of questions regarding their source of income and personal information. Amounts from Guaranteed Income Supplement, Canada Pension Plan (or Quebec Pension Plan), Old Age Security, and other related programs are input by CCRA based on a respondent's answers.

If successful, the program may be expanded to include people who have simple returns and low income (such as those who are on social assistance, or those who receive only a GST-refundable tax credit).

AUDITS

Where the word *taxes* makes us groan, the very idea of an audit can turn our stomachs. Visions of stiff-necked, starchy suited people sifting through our lives can cause indigestion for even the bravest of souls. The truth is, most of us will never even be audited (high-income earners and the self-employed are more likely to achieve this dubious honour). And if you've filed accurate returns based on your neatly organized, equally accurate records, then an audit is really more of an inconvenience than anything.

Who Does CCRA Audit?

CCRA can audit anyone at random. Usually, however, they're looking for "red flags," signs that all is not what it seems with a return:

- Poor record-keeping

- Income sources such as commission

- "Hot" deductions, such as losses from entertainment industry investments

- Third-party informants

If CCRA does select you for an audit, an auditor will contact you to arrange a convenient time to meet. Be prepared! This includes being confident, organized, and informed. I have a friend named William who gets audited every year. Fortunately for him, he finds the audit a challenge and reads up on the Income Tax Act every year to prepare for the audit. Unless you're like William, even if you've done your tax returns yourself, you should have a bookkeeper or accountant go over your return(s) with you beforehand, then have them attend the audit meeting with you so they can explain anything that you can't. Your stomach will thank you!

If You Are Audited

Take all your receipts, cancelled cheques, books, records, and invoices with you, along with copies of everything for the tax preparer. That way, if the tax preparer loses some of your material, you can back up your position with your copies so that you're not losing out on some of your deductions.

Be polite and professional with the CCRA auditor. Auditors are only doing their jobs, and it's in your best interests not to antagonize them. Respect will ensure the job gets done as quickly and painlessly as possible. Argument will ensure the exact opposite.

Once the audit is complete, the auditor will decide whether to reassess you or accept your return. He or she can continue to reassess until satisfied with the return's accuracy. When you receive the assessment, and if you agree with it, you'll have to pay any amount due. If that amount is more than you can reasonably handle, you can request a payment plan. Providing a series of postdated cheques will show CCRA that you intend to fulfill your obligations, and it will make sure that you don't forget an upcoming payment.

If you disagree with the audit results, you can try to work out a solution with the auditor. Alternatively, you can file a Notice of Objection within 90 days of the new assessment. The objection must be in writing and detail why you think the assessment is wrong or unfair (a formal Notice of Objection, called a T400A, is available from your local tax office). Once CCRA has reviewed your objection, you'll be asked either to attend a meeting with an appeals officer (you should take your accountant or legal representative with you), or to provide further information in writing.

If you cannot reach an agreement with the appeals officer, CCRA will either confirm your assessment or change it. Either way, you'll receive notification by registered mail. If you're still unsatisfied with the assessment, you have a further 90 days to file another Notice of Objection, or you can appeal the assessment to the Tax Court of Canada. If you choose the latter approach, legal representation is not required, but it is highly recommended.

CHAPTER SUMMARY

- Not everyone must file a return, but if you do, ensure you do so by the filing deadline.

  - Penalties and interest

  - Late filing need-to-knows

  - Notice of assessment

- Take advantage of any and all tax-saving strategies:

  - Deductions

  - Tax credits

  - Excluded benefits

  - Tax planning

- Your other tax responsibilities include maintaining precise records for seven years.

- You can make changes to already-filed returns.

- NETFILE and other CCRA services will help you file easier.

- Audits are a serious thing, but can be more of an inconvenience than anything if you're prepared.

Balancing Your Kids

Sharing Your Financial Health

"Tell me and I will forget. Show me and I may remember.
Involve me and I will understand."
—Chinese Proverb

You already know that children learn a great deal by example. Eat well, stay active, and chances are that your child will follow suit. Live on chips, pop, and ice cream while glued to the television, and guess what? Couch potato children!

But real education does not stop with example only. For a child to form truly healthy lifestyle habits, he or she must not just observe, but be allowed to participate. It's not enough to put a plate of vegetables in front of your child every night; he won't truly adopt healthy eating habits for himself unless he participates in the choices and the preparation. Likewise for exercise: Having your child see you go off to an aerobics class every evening will never replace sharing a long walk or bike ride with her—and actually including her in an active lifestyle.

Your kids will learn about finances in much the same way. Some of it they will absorb through observation. A child who has watched her parents adopt a healthy attitude toward savings may take that attitude with her even after leaving home; and a child who has learned by example to delay gratification will be far less inclined to buy into the have-it-all-now mentality once he or she ventures out alone.

But observation alone won't give children the tools they need to effectively plan and control their own financial futures, and they don't teach money management in either grade school or high school, so it's up to us to make sure that our children have the learning opportunities they need.

SUCCESS TIP

Start early!

- Buy a piggy bank for your child to save loose change in.
- Explain that an ATM is like their piggy bank . You have to put money in before you can take it out.
- Let them use loose change to play "store" and help them become familiar with the denominations.
- Let them pay for small purchases at the store and explain what "change" is.

Think about your own experiences as a child. Chances are that if you've found yourself struggling with your own finances throughout your life, your own introduction to money management was somewhat less than complete. And chances are, too, that if you're like most parents, you want something better for your own kids. You don't want them to have to learn all their lessons the hard way; you want them to have a better start, with a better education and a brighter financial future.

The good news is that giving your kids that better start isn't as difficult as you might think. Simply including them in your own financial planning process—and in your decision-making—will pay huge dividends for them down the road.

SUCCESS TIP

Look for hidden opportunities to teach your kids about money. Even a trip to the grocery store can be a lesson in choices and priorities.

Obviously I'm not talking about letting your kids make the actual decisions about whether or not you need a new vehicle, or if you can afford a family vacation this year. Those decisions are, and should remain, yours alone. But the simple act of letting your children participate in your planning process will drive home lessons that they may never otherwise acquire—at least not until they're having to make such decisions for themselves, with no idea how to begin—lessons like setting priorities, postponing or sacrificing wants in order to deal first with needs, and considering alternatives.

A general family discussion about financial goals will encourage your kids to work with you toward a major purchase, and give them a real sense of teamwork and accomplishment that will form a solid foundation for their own future financial endeavours.

Similarly, an open approach to dealing with suddenly shrinking family finances (due to the loss of a job, or the need to pay down a large debt load, for example) can teach children how to deal with financial situations that are less than rosy.

Of course, if your own money-management skills leave something to be desired, you don't necessarily want to pass your own habits on to your children. Likewise, a complex financial system that includes multiple investment and savings strategies might only serve to confuse your children, especially if they're younger. So keep things simple when you start out, and be sure that what you teach them is what you want them to retain throughout their lives, because retain it they will.

> ### *SUCCESS TIP*
> Don't be afraid to say no. Kids need to understand that parents have limited resources, and very young children often won't even remember their impulse demands.

An easy way to reinforce good money management skills, regardless of how involved your children are in the family financial picture, is by way of an allowance. (If you don't believe in paying an allowance, consider the tips in *Payment for Odd Jobs* later in this chapter.)

ALLOWANCES

As parents, we are responsible for seeing to our children's needs and many of their wants: We clothe them, feed them, purchase their school materials, give them toys, pay for extras such as baseball, ballet, or other activities, and we're usually ready to open our pockets when a handful of change (or more) is requested.

> ### Top 10 Reasons to Give Your Child an Allowance
> 1. They'll learn the value of money.
> 2. They'll learn how to budget.
> 3. Any mistakes they make will be minimal (instead of costing thousands of dollars when they're older).
> 4. They'll learn to consider the cost of things.
> 5. They'll learn to make spending choices.
> 6. They'll learn to prioritize their needs and wants.
> 7. They'll be less likely to be drawn in by a marketing pitch if they have to pay for an item themselves.

8. They'll have more appreciation for things they've paid for themselves.

9. They'll learn about delayed gratification by having to save for big-ticket items.

10. It takes the pressure off you: It will no longer be a matter of whether or not you can afford something, but whether or not *they* can.

It doesn't take long for most kids to equate our money with their own satisfaction. Who among us hasn't had to deal with demands, whining, and tantrums that are all geared towards the gratification of our child's wants? Even if we involve our children in our family budget sessions and become adept at telling them that we can't afford to appease their every whim, simple experience remains our child's best teacher and a parent's best ally. There's nothing like a regular income, paired with having to make tough spending choices, to teach real fiscal responsibility.

Setting the Rules

There are nearly as many ways of handling allowances as there are families raising children, so you'll have to decide for yourself what works for your family. Some people tie allowances into household chores, feeling that this instills the concept of earning; others think that the two should be separate and that a child should contribute to household chores because he's a part of the family and not because he's paid to do so (if you don't get paid to do the laundry, why should your child be paid to clean his room?). You'll need to decide which approach best fits your family values and philosophies.

Whatever your system, make sure it's consistent, and make sure your child knows the rules. If the allowance is tied to chores, be specific. What chores, exactly? If you're paying an allowance simply because your child is a member of the family and you want her to learn money management, tell her so.

Decide what you expect your child's allowance to cover. This could vary with your child's age and ability to handle responsibility. For instance, a younger child could be expected to purchase her own comic books, while an older child might be asked to pay for her own entertainment costs (movies, concerts, etc.). Think about whether or not the child will be responsible for buying gifts for family members and/or friends. What about saving up for longer-term things, such as vacation spending money? Make sure your child knows what the expectations are.

SUCCESS TIP

An allowance can go a long way to teaching fiscal responsibility that is better learned now (with small amounts) than later, when poor money habits can create serious problems.

How Much?

There are varying opinions on how to determine the amount of an allowance. Some people pay a dollar per year of age (a three-year-old would get $3, a 10-year-old would get $10, etc.); others pay whatever the "going rate" is. Your most important consideration will be how much you can comfortably afford. Even if that's considerably less than the "going rate," you're not trying to keep up with the Joneses, remember?

Here are some other considerations when you're deciding where to set an allowance:

• How much are you currently spending on your child's wants? Try tracking your spending for a couple of weeks to see what you're actually forking over for your child's demands. You may want to start the allowance at that amount, or you may be shocked to find you're spending a lot more than you thought, in which case you'll probably want to start lower.

- How old is your child? A five-year-old won't have the same spending needs—or wants—as a 13-year-old. Likewise, a three-year-old may be satisfied with enough allowance to buy his own package of gum once a week.

- What is the allowance expected to cover? Is this simply mad money, or do you expect your child to cover certain expenses?

- Do you want the child to contribute to a long-term savings plan out of the allowance amount?

- Do you want to teach charity as well? Having a child set aside a small amount from each allowance can instill a lifetime habit of giving to those less fortunate.

How Often?

Many people opt to pay their kids on their own paydays. Keep in mind, however, that bi-weekly can seem like an eternity for a very young child; little minds will cope much more easily with weekly payments.

SUCCESS TIP

Pay allowances in smaller denominations that can be easily divided up into the categories you and your child have decided on. It's easier for a child to immediately put a toonie into a charity or savings envelope than it is to remember to hold $2 back from the $10 bill burning a hole in his pocket!

Once you've committed to a frequency, pay on time! Not only does this make your child's budgeting education a lot easier, it also subtly underlines the importance you place on honouring your own financial obligations.

When?

Experts vary in their opinions about when a child should start receiving an allowance. Most agree that by the age of seven or eight, an allowance is a critical factor in learning good money management; many advocate starting even younger than that.

I like the approach that recommends giving an allowance when a child is old enough to comprehend the exchange of money for goods—usually at about age three. By this time, kids are equating the shiny stuff in your pocket with the ability to get their hands on that coveted toy or candy bar, and they're ready to begin learning the value of coins (they may not understand that a quarter is worth 25 cents, but they'll catch on fast to the idea of exchanging four of those quarters for a package of candy).

Even if your child is older, it's not too late to begin giving an allowance, or to start them on the road to financial savvy.

Increases

Your system of allowance should be flexible enough to allow for your child's changing needs as he or she grows. You should review the amount regularly with your child (at least once a year), at which time you can offer a standard yearly increase to reflect your child's increased needs (and inflation), or you can have your child show why such an increase is justified (she could document increased prices, or indicate a willingness to take on additional financial responsibilities).

Dealing with a Child's Financial Disasters

When you first start giving an allowance, chances are pretty good that your child will spend it all at the beginning of the week, leaving nothing left over for the remaining days (sound familiar?). Expect this, and stand firm. Remember that if you're consistently there to bail your child out of his financial tight spots, the only thing you'll be teaching him is that he can always rely on you to do so (not such a big thing when it's a $10 allowance, but a little more serious when it's a several-thousand-dollar car loan!).

If you do feel the need to "help" your child out, do so on a business footing. Lend the money for necessities (wants are different, and could provide an opportunity to underline a lesson in delayed gratification), but expect to be repaid and be sure that your child understands the repayment terms. Put it in writing and have your child sign it. It will be something that he or she will remember. If your child is older and the allowance overspending becomes a habit (perpetuated by the convenience of having built-in lenders, i.e., you), you could also charge a nominal amount of interest. It's better for your child to find out the real cost of credit with you now, and not with a professional lender down the road.

Big-Ticket Items

When it comes to saving for a big-ticket item, we're all familiar with the "it feels like forever" syndrome. This is even truer for the younger set. If a child has to meet certain expenses from her $10 a week, saving $400 for horseback riding camp can take two years or more. Try to resist the temptation to rush in and "rescue" your child whenever the going seems to get tough. Remember, you're trying to instill lifetime habits here.

If the item your child chooses to save for is something you consider worthwhile, and you'd like to contribute to their efforts, you can do so in two ways:

• A savings-matching program (you contribute a dollar for each dollar they save on their own)

• Payment for odd jobs (outside of the expected household obligations)

For younger children who aren't able to take on larger, physical tasks, a savings-matching program is probably the better solution. Offer to pay for a portion of the item if your child pays for the rest. This can be done on a 50-50 ratio, or whatever split you prefer.

Payment for Odd Jobs

Paying your child to do odd jobs can serve two purposes: It can help your child towards a long-term savings goal, and it can also foster an entrepreneurial spirit.

SUCCESS TIP

You can pay your child to do odd jobs in order to supplement an allowance, or in place of one if you prefer not to go the allowance route.

What constitutes an odd job? Anything that your child isn't expected to do on a regular basis as a part of his or her chores, whether or not those chores are tied in to allowance. Odd jobs are the extras that crop up on occasion—painting the fence, washing the car, stacking the winter's supply of firewood, etc. These jobs are often something you'd hire someone else to do...so why not hire your own kids?

Start by having them do work around your own home, so that you can provide guidance and ensure that they learn to do a thorough job, and then let them move on to offering their services to neighbours and friends.

Who Controls the Spending?

The most difficult challenge you'll face in teaching your children about money management is letting them make mistakes. The temptation to rush in and rescue them from overspending or from an improvident purchase will be strong...resist it. How they spend their allowance is up to them, not you. You can set the parameters (expenses they're expected to pay for), and you can offer advice (show them how you budget your own money), but you cannot make their decisions for them.

Remember: Trial and error is an important component of learning for kids, just like it is for us. The key difference is that their mistakes will be a lot less costly if they make them now instead of later.

SAVINGS PROGRAMS AND BANK ACCOUNTS

Healthy eating habits are best learned, and certainly more easily learned, early in life. The same goes for healthy savings habits. If you haven't already started your child on a savings program, do so. Now. Because learning to save is probably the most critical component of smart money management.

SUCCESS TIP

Splurging occasionally on ourselves or others is an important part of living. Remember that the idea is to give your child "money smarts"—enough knowledge and guidance to develop healthy money skills while still enjoying life.

Regardless of whether or not you choose to pay an allowance to your children, at some point they will have money of their own (birthday gifts, odd jobs, etc.). A portion of any money passing through their hands should be devoted to savings.

Setting up a Savings Program

Saving doesn't need to be complicated. For example, depending on your personal views, you could:

• Require that a certain percentage of all funds be deposited into a bank account

• Allow your child to spend bills but save all her change

• Have your child save part of his allowance and job money, but let him spend all of his birthday money

Explain to them that saving is simply postponed spending. They'll still be able to spend the money, just not now, and not on impulse buys. It helps, too, if you give them a reason for saving, something concrete that they're aiming for. Small children could save for a particular toy that they'd like; an older one could save for a bike, or perhaps music lessons.

Some families prefer to break savings down into short and long term. Short-term savings are used towards the larger-ticket wants, and the long-term savings are set aside for something further down the road, such as university tuition.

When Should Your Child Open a Bank Account?

You can open a bank account for a child at any time, but depending on the type of account, you may need to guarantee it until your child reaches the age of majority (either 18 or 19, depending on your province). Because a child can't legally be held to a contract (such as a chequing account), banks will sometimes require an adult to be the legal "owner" of the account. If you must, open the account jointly with your child, and then remove your own name when your child is of age. CIBC has an excellent Web site detailing bank accounts at www2.cibc.com/smartstart. The site also has great information and games that help teach finances to kids of all ages.

Bear in mind that while an older child will be comfortable depositing funds into a bank account (they understand that their money is still there, even if they can't see it), very young children can have serious issues with handing over their shiny coins to a stranger. For younger kids, then, a more visible savings "account" is often better.

SUCCESS TIP

- Make saving easier by making goals specific: "I want to attend veterinary college in Guelph" is a lot more concrete than "I want to go to university someday"—especially if it's accompanied by a picture of the university in Guelph!

• Plot success on a graph or chart: "Look, I've saved $200 of the $400 I need for horseback riding camp!"

One family I know began with three jars for each of their children at age four. Come allowance day, one-third of the money went into long-term savings for university, one-third went into short-terms savings for special items (including expenses such as family gifts), and the last third was mad money for immediate spending (required to last, of course, until the next allowance day). Once their children were old enough to understand the function of a bank, the contents of the long-term savings jars were transferred into individual bank savings accounts.

In my own family, each of my children has a personal bank account, with a passbook that they keep in a resealable plastic bag. When they have money to put into their accounts, the money goes into the plastic bag with the passbook until the next trip to the bank. My kids love to check their passbooks to see how much interest they've earned, and what their balances are.

TWEENS AND TEENS

Just as most other things become more challenging when our kids reach a certain age, finances are no different. Peer pressure, growing independence, and (hopefully) increased responsibility all play roles in the changing financial situations of our tweens and teens.

Peer Pressure

Peer pressure is enormously powerful. Even if you have never struggled to keep up with the Joneses yourself, you may still find your kids swayed by peer influence. The right clothes, the right stereo equipment, even the right computer can become issues for kids who are struggling to find their own identity and declare their independence from you.

If you haven't already discussed marketing issues with your kids, now is a really good time to do so. Talk to them about fads and marketing ploys, and be honest about your family's financial circumstances. Sure, we'd all like to be as rich as that popular kid's family, but the truth is that we're not, and there's no shame in the fact.

SUCCESS TIP

Search out alternatives: Consignment stores can yield a treasure trove of "in" items. If you haven't already explored these stores, why not check them out, with your tween or teen in tow, of course!

Try to find a middle ground. Understand your tween's or teen's need to fit in, but stand firm on your spending principles. Don't be swayed by tears or attempted guilt trips ("But Melissa's mom bought her these running shoes!"). And if your children really want an item badly enough, tell them they're welcome to save for it. It's amazing how quickly a "need" for a designer shirt is forgotten when it comes time to fork over the $120 plus taxes to pay for it!

Growing Independence

As your children get older, chances are that they will be off doing more things without you...like going to movies with friends, eating out at restaurants, and going to concerts. It stands to reason that their expenses will increase accordingly. Even if you're able to manage an allowance increase, don't be afraid to encourage them to think outside the box when it comes to earning money for themselves.

Kids as young as nine or 10 are able to rake leaves for a neighbour, or to offer a dog-walking service. By age 12, a child can take up babysitting or lawn and garden maintenance; by 16, they can be stocking shelves at the local grocery store or pharmacy (but remember, once they're employed, they also have to begin submitting tax returns).

Increased Responsibility

If you think your tweens or teens are up to the challenge, let them take more responsibility for their own expenses. For instance, decide how much you might spend on a back-to-school wardrobe, and give the money to your child so that she can do her own shopping. You may be pleasantly surprised to find how creative she can be once she realizes how far those funds have to go. On the other hand, she may also claim that she's happy to wash and wear the same pair of "in" jeans every day for months, in which case try to grin and bear it, and don't be tempted to buy her another pair.

Premature Affluence

Whether it's through the generosity of grandparents, an above-average-wage job, or the success of an entrepreneurial undertaking, some kids can find themselves with more money on their hands than is good for them. This, in turn, can lead to a dream world of discretionary spending (what I want, I buy), and could result in other irresponsible behaviours, such as alcohol, drugs, and gambling. If you're not happy with your teens' overly rosy financial situation, here are three ways to limit their discretion:

• Control their expenditures by disallowing purchases. The opposite viewpoint to this is letting them discover for themselves the consequences of spending all their money on their discretionary purchases.

• Impose extra savings requirements. The 10-per-cent savings rule that made sense when their allowance was only a few dollars a week may no longer apply if they're earning megabucks at a job (and expecting you to finance their university education).

• Room and board clawbacks. Some parents have difficulty charging their children for room and board. A solution might be to have them increase their education savings instead, with the stipulation that if they decide not to attend university (but want to remain at home), they'll have to start paying room and board at that time.

Credit Cards for Teens

Some experts are in favour of letting a teen have a credit card. I'm not. It's like letting them have an all-you-can-eat pizza, milkshake, and tower-of-power cheesecake diet.

The "expert" justification is that if teens don't have credit cards, they won't know how to use them. You could say the same thing about a gun, but given the dangers involved, I'd rather explain how a gun works than buy my son a firearm.

The idea that a credit card is a learning experience for a teen simply does not make sense to me. Controlling credit card use is highly challenging for most adults. It seems irrational to expect teens, who don't have the benefit of experience and who face more extreme pressures to consume than their parents, to be more disciplined than adults about credit card use. Surely we can teach credit card fundamentals without actually giving credit!

If possible, credit card use in teen years should be avoided. For those of you who choose to disregard this advice, however, you should at least take measures to limit the potential damage that can result:

- Consider starting your teen off with a debit card rather than a credit card. Make the possibility of future credit contingent on responsible use of the debit card. Be careful when setting up this account. If it links to your own, you could be in for a nasty surprise!

- Check out the "specialty" credit cards such as "secured cards" or "stored-value cards." Aimed at the teen market, these are prepaid cards that function like credit cards, but require the deposit of funds (usually by the parent or grandparent).

- Avoid "real" credit cards (Visa, Mastercard, etc.). If your child is under the age of majority, you'll have to co-sign for the card, making you legally responsible for any debt that your child incurs. If you do go this route, keep the limit low, and make sure the credit card company doesn't "helpfully" increase the limit without your consent.

- Don't add your child's name to your own credit card. With your higher credit limit, you're inviting trouble, and there's also a higher likelihood that your child's card will be lost or stolen, resulting in major inconvenience and expense for you.

Before you consent to credit for your teen, it's crucial that you talk to them about the dangers involved. Explain how interest compounds on unpaid balances, how making only minimum payments can exorbitantly increase the true cost of an item (see Chapter Two), and how a tarnished credit rating can hamper their future ability to establish themselves financially. Then, and only then, if you're still certain that you want your teen (and you) to take this route, be sure you establish clear-cut rules about credit limits, repayment, and default procedures.

You know how serious credit is, and how quickly too much of it can ruin your debt diet; be sure your teen does, too.

CHAPTER SUMMARY

- Setting an example for your children is how they'll learn. Involving them, however, helps them learn faster and better.

- Allowances, when structured properly for your family, can help you teach the value of money.

- Savings programs and bank accounts teach the needs-versus-wants argument.

- When your children become tweens and teens, they are at the age they can begin learning about the more complex financial concepts of credit and budgeting.

CHAPTER TEN

Taking Care of the Future

Planning for Financial Success

"If you would be wealthy, think of saving as well as getting."
—Benjamin Franklin

If a diet is to be successful, it cannot be about weight loss alone; it must also be about making long-term lifestyle changes that involve more than simple calorie cutbacks. Altering your approach to nutrition and health requires both foresight and planning, and altering your approach to finances requires exactly the same.

Once a budget has put you and your family on the right track (you're losing debt weight), you need a way to make sure that you stay on track. That's the foresight part. And once you've set long-term goals for yourself, such as a child's education or your own retirement, you need a way to reach those goals. That's the planning part. Bear in mind that you can move forward to this stage only once the debt issues have been largely dealt with. Otherwise, these goals will seem very daunting and unattainable.

FORESIGHT: GUARDING AGAINST DIETARY SETBACKS

Remember those vegetables that you hated when you were growing up, but your mother made you eat them because they were good for you? Some aspects of financial planning might seem just as unpalatable, but they're just as necessary to good financial health as vegetables are to your nutritional health. While you might prefer to avoid thinking about things like estate planning and life insurance, you seriously jeopardize your entire family's financial future if you don't look after them.

Estate Planning

The idea of planning for your own death can be both unsettling and unnerving, but if you care about the people in your life, then for their sake you must have a will. A will is a legal document that speaks for you when you no longer can. It sets out who you want to have your assets, and who you want to look after your child(ren) after your death.

Without a will, you are said to have died "intestate," and your assets will be divided according to the laws of the province in which you reside, with no regard for how you might have wanted things done. These laws vary from province to province, but usually mean that your assets are split between your legal wife/husband and child(ren), with other close blood relatives sometimes included, as well. Common-law spouses can be excluded entirely. For a snapshot of how your estate will be distributed if you die without a will, see Appendix "E".

Another serious concern if you die intestate is that your assets (referred to as your "estate") are distributed immediately and administered by the government. This means that if a substantial share of your estate is designated for your child before he or she is ready to handle that kind of money, it will be a government official who handles your child's affairs rather than a relative or friend.

And if you're still not convinced that you need a will, consider these points:

• Dying intestate usually means higher income taxes are paid on the estate, leaving less to be distributed.

• Legal fees are also higher.

- Your survivors must seek appointment by the court to be the Estate Administrator if they want to administer your estate.

- Court-appointed administrators, in trying to do their jobs, might subject your family to additional stresses during a difficult time.

- If you don't name a guardian, your children could end up in foster care if your relatives are unable or unwilling to take care of them.

Drawing up a Will

While do-it-yourself will kits are readily available, and that option is certainly better than none, I strongly recommend you have your will drawn up by a qualified wills and estates lawyer in your province (in Quebec, you'll use a notary). A do-it-yourself will might be cheaper than a lawyer, but you still need to observe the same legal formalities, such as witnesses, and the potential exists for making a serious mistake, especially if you think that there might be a dispute about how you want your estate to be distributed.

The Cost of a Will

The cost of having a legal will drawn up varies according to your circumstances (the more complex your affairs, the more you'll pay), but expect to pay at least $250. If you and your spouse draw up wills at the same time, you may be able to get a package deal from your lawyer or notary.

Before you meet with a lawyer (or notary), you'll need to give some consideration to certain key points:

1. *Who do you want to be your executor?*

    - An executor, or executrix (also known as an estate trustee in some provinces), is a person you name in your will to oversee the administration of your estate. He or she will see that your estate is distributed according to your wishes, and that any outstanding debts, taxes, fees, etc., are paid. Be sure to name an alternate executor in the event that the first named executor is unable or unwilling to act.

- Your executor may need to make decisions about things that you haven't covered in your will, so choose someone whose judgment you trust and who is experienced in financial matters.

- Consider other characteristics, such as organization and age, as well. You should choose someone either similar in age or younger than yourself (who will likely outlive you), and who can handle the complexity of the job in a time of grief.

- Your executor should *not* be the same person as the guardian you choose for your child(ren). An independent executor can—and should—act as a safety check for your children's financial welfare.

- Your executor should live in the same province as you, and in the same area if possible, in order to reduce costs to your estate (for travel, accommodation, etc.).

- If you don't think that one person can handle all of the details, you can appoint more than one executor. In appointing more than one, consider appointing an odd number (usually three), so that if there is a dispute among executors, the decision of the majority will prevail.

- Just because a person is named as an executor in a will doesn't mean that he/she is legally obliged to take on the task, so talk to your chosen executor *before* writing your will to be sure that he/she is willing to accept the position.

- Your executor will be paid a fee from the estate for this work (up to five per cent of the estate's value).

- If you can't think of someone to appoint as executor, you can use a lawyer, accountant, or trust company instead.

2. *Who should you appoint as guardian?*

- If both you and your spouse die while your children are still minors (under age 18 or 19, depending the province you live in), you need to think about who you'd like your children to live with until they are of legal age. Your goal here is to make a devastating trauma in your children's lives as easy for them as you possibly can (even though it will never be easy), so consider your choices carefully and always with your children's best interests in mind.

- Choose guardians that you trust to parent in a similar way to you. Guardians don't need to be relatives, so consider close friends as well.

- Consider factors such as compatibility. Do your children like the guardians you're considering? Do the potential guardians like your kids? Do they already have kids of their own, and if so, can they handle the addition of yours into their family? Can *their* kids handle it? Can yours?

- Think about location. Your children will already be going through a very difficult time: Would they be able to handle being uprooted from all that is familiar and sent to the other side of the country?

- Be aware that even if you appoint a guardian in your will, that appointment is not legally binding—a court still makes the final decision. The court will, however, find your wishes very persuasive. For that reason, if there is someone that you absolutely do *not* want to raise your child, you probably want to specify this.

- Be sure to specify an alternate choice of guardian also, in case your first choice is unable or unwilling to fulfill the appointment at the time of your death.

When you meet with your lawyer/notary, you'll need to have certain information and documents on hand. There are numerous estate planner checklists found in estate and financial guides, but here are some of the things you'll want to have ready for your appointment:

- *Assets.* Make a list of all your bank accounts, RRSPs, investments, pensions, Canada Savings Bonds, safety deposit boxes, house deeds, etc. (along with any pertinent information, such as location and amount), and take the information with you to your appointment. You might want to leave a copy of this list with your lawyer, or at least place a copy of it with your will once it's drawn up.

- *Sentimental Items.* Make a list of things that you want given to specific people (jewellery, art objects, etc.). Your lawyer will include these in a "specific bequests" paragraph in your will to ensure your wishes are followed. The description of these items should be specific so that there is no doubt about which items they are. Consider including photographs for confirmation, especially when the items are jewellery or art objects.

- *Life Insurance Policies.* List all of your policies, their amounts, and their beneficiaries. Don't make your estate your beneficiary; instead, specify the beneficiaries. Insurance proceeds that are paid into an estate are subject to probate fees, while those that are paid to named beneficiaries are usually not. The exception to this rule is in Quebec: Life insurance proceeds there are *not* subject to probate fees.

- *RRSPs.* Again, name a specific beneficiary and an alternate to avoid having the proceeds pass through the estate where they'll attract taxes and probate fees (if your spouse is the beneficiary, he/she can receive the proceeds directly through a tax rollover). For more information, speak to an accountant, financial advisor, or lawyer.

Distinct Difference

Jointly held property in most provinces automatically passes to the survivor(s) if one of the joint owners dies. In Quebec, however, joint property is automatically frozen until the will is probated and the deceased's wishes regarding his/her portion of the property are known. This includes joint bank accounts, real estate, and other assets. If you live in Quebec but your bank accounts originate in another province, such as Ontario, however, the accounts won't be frozen because the other province's rules apply to them.

Once your will is drawn up and finalized, be sure to keep a copy of it in a safe place, such as a fireproof safe in your home. Your lawyer will usually keep the original. A safety deposit box is not a good idea because it will be sealed if you die, making it extremely difficult for the executor to get at your will. Wherever you decide to keep your will, make sure that your executor knows where to find it.

You should review your will every three to five years, or whenever there is a major change in your life (such as a birth or death) or financial circumstances. An important note here is that if you remarry, your prior will is automatically revoked in most provinces. The same automatic revocation does *not* happen, however, on divorce. If you are separating or getting divorced, one of the first things you should do is change your will. Failure to do so may result in your ex-spouse receiving a windfall that you might have preferred he/she didn't get.

And finally, do your executor an enormous favour by keeping your financial affairs and paperwork in order and readily available if something should happen to you. This can be as simple as keeping a binder on hand—and updating it periodically—with all the information your executor will need regarding assets, investments, insurance policies, debts, etc. Without this information, your executor could face a long and frustrating job of tracking down the details, and might not even be able to find everything. This could mean delays in the distribution of your estate, and even result in lawsuits by creditors and others.

Powers of Attorney

In addition to having your will drawn up, you also need to have your lawyer or notary draw up powers of attorney. These are legal documents that grant another person the right to make decisions for you if you are mentally or physically incapacitated (in a coma or suffering from Alzheimer's, for instance), but still alive. In addition, a power of attorney can, if specified, also give another person the right to manage your affairs for you while you're still capable of doing so yourself (useful if you'll be out of the country and need someone to take care of business transactions for you in your absence).

Powers of attorney are usually broken down into two types: one for property, and another for personal care. A power of attorney for property will let the other person make decisions regarding your money or property; without one, your spouse or dependants will have to go to court to get an order letting them manage your affairs.

A power of attorney for personal care, or living will, lets the appointed person make medical decisions for you when you can no longer do so yourself (such as end-of-life decisions).

You should review your powers of attorney regularly, and update them whenever you update your will. Note that, unlike prior wills, powers of attorney are *not* always automatically revoked in the case of remarriage—check this with your lawyer!

SUCCESS TIP

Have your powers of attorney drawn up at the same time as your will. Most lawyers will include it in their fee for doing the will. If you have a power of attorney drawn up separately, it will cost you $100 to $200.

Life Insurance

Third on the list of must-haves in order to secure your family's future: life insurance. The purpose of life insurance is to insure your life so that the people who depend on your income (or on your housekeeping and child-rearing skills) won't be left high and dry in the event of your death. It's another of those rather unpalatable thoughts, but unless you're very wealthy, it's critical.

The life insurance industry has grown and changed tremendously in the last few decades, and the traditional, simple policy that pays out on the sudden death of an insured is now only part of the picture. Life insurance is often an integral part of your savings plan, investments, cash flow, or personal approach to risk. Accordingly, you need to ensure you can make sense of what's being offered, and then make decisions based on what's best for you and your family.

Term insurance remains the simplest approach, with your life insured for a set period, or "term" (e.g., until you reach the age of 65). Once the term expires, your coverage ends unless you renew it (assuming the policy allows for a renewal). One of the big advantages of term insurance is that the substantially lower premiums enable you to purchase sufficient coverage to protect against loss of income. Any discretionary investment funds can be placed in other vehicles, such as mutual funds (money market accounts that are likely to generate returns similar to or better than life insurance policies).

You may view term insurance policies as wasted money, because you don't get any return on your "investment." However, term policies are insurance in the truest sense of the word, much like vehicle insurance or house insurance. They can help cover the loss of income, funeral, and other expenses in the event of death. They can also assist your family to maintain the current lifestyle if there is a sudden loss.

SUCCESS TIP

If you have a large mortgage and can afford only one insurance policy, consider getting your life insurance through a life insurance company instead of the bank or trust company. It could be a cheaper way of retiring your house debt in the event of your death. If you and your spouse are jointly insured and die together, the amount is paid twice, effectively paying off the house and providing money to your dependants. With a financial institution insurance policy, the insurance coverage decreases as the outstanding mortgage decreases.

Whole life, or permanent, insurance policies insure you for your lifetime. There is no set term, no expiry, and no need to renegotiate. A part of the premium is applied toward insuring your life while the other part goes toward an investment account. This investment account can either be an interest-bearing account or a stocks-and-bonds investment account. The advantage of whole life is that you can cash in your policy and receive the cash surrender value of it, or borrow against its value, usually at lower than bank interest rates.

Universal life insurance combines term life insurance with an investment account. Various costs, including administration expenses, are withdrawn from the term premiums and the investment account, with the balance invested in money market funds.

Universal premiums can increase or decrease, and be paid on an irregular schedule as long as enough money remains in the account to cover the above-mentioned costs. Universal provides a tax-free death benefit and some tax-shelter possibilities, along with a growing investment income.

Variable life insurance is another hybrid, this one combining permanent whole life insurance with a fixed premium. An investment component in a segregated fund is invested much the way mutual funds are in equity, bond, or balanced funds. There is a guaranteed return of contributions depending on how long you leave the investment portion in place, making it slightly more secure than mutual funds. As with universal life insurance, variable life carries a tax-free death benefit and limited tax-shelter possibilities.

Disability Insurance

One-third of adults aged 35 or older will be disabled for at least six months before reaching age 65. Hard to believe, but true. Whether you're employed by someone else, or self-employed, if your family relies upon your income to meet household expenses or to cover loan or mortgage payments (and whose family doesn't?), you need to have disability insurance that pays a minimum of 60 per cent of your income. If you're employed, you may already be covered through an employee, union, or professional association plan; however, chances are that you're still *under*insured.

Few group disability plans are generous enough to meet your needs, and most are "any job" plans, which means that if the insurance company thinks that you're employable in any capacity (not necessarily your normal job), they can cut you off. Group plans also terminate if you're laid off or quit, so it's wise to have a parallel personal plan in place while you're working. If and when you're no longer with your employer, you can increase the personal plan as needed.

Disability insurance premiums can seem exorbitant, especially if you're self-employed, but if you weigh them against the catastrophic effects of finding yourself without an income for any length of time, they suddenly take on a new perspective. Shop around, do your homework, and ask questions to find the best policy *and* the best rate. The Canadian Life and Health Insurance Association offers assistance with this through a free guide called *Disability Insurance: Where Will the Money Come From If You're Disabled?*, available from its Web site at www.clhia.ca.

Household Insurance

More insurance? Yes, but remember, vegetables are good for you! Household insurance (also called home, tenants', occupiers', or property and casualty insurance) is another in the list of "must-haves" if you want to secure your financial future.

SUCCESS TIP

If you have a home office, be sure to inform your insurer. Home policies exclude property damage and third-party liability that relate to your business; you need either a separate home business policy or a "rider" on your home policy to cover these losses and liabilities.

Whether you own or rent, you need a minimum amount of insurance: contents if you rent, home and contents if you own, and third-party liability regardless. Your belongings can be insured for replacement or depreciated value, with the latter being cheaper (but not necessarily smarter if you lose something and need to replace it). Even if you have a replacement value policy, you'll only get the replacement value if you actually buy a replacement item. If you ask for a cash payout on something, chances are that you'll get a cheque for the depreciated value. My advice is to get replacement cost insurance—it costs more but the benefits far exceed the costs.

Third-party liability insurance is essential for protection in the event that you're sued for damages. I recommend that you have at least $2 million of this type of coverage. Anything lower and you will probably be underinsured, which means that if you're found liable and are underinsured, you'll have to make up the difference from your own pocket.

When insuring your home, resist the temptation to overinsure. Insured property includes only the building, and not the land that lies under it. To decide how much insurance you need for the contents of your home, do an inventory of your possessions (don't forget to include provincial sales tax, goods and services tax, or harmonized tax when you're figuring out values). Update your inventory list once a year, and change your coverage as needed. Also consider photographing or videotaping the contents of your home on a yearly basis. Keep the information in your safety deposit box or in a safe place off-site. If you store the pictures or video at home and there is a fire, hurricane, or other disaster, you will have potentially lost your valuable records.

The key thing to be aware of when insuring your home is that policies differ from company to company. Again, ask questions, be informed, and shop around.

PLANNING: LOOKING AHEAD TO A HEALTHY FINANCIAL FUTURE

Leaving those unpalatable vegetables behind now, and moving along to more savoury topics, it's time to consider your goals for your children's education and your own retirement, and to plan how you'll comfortably achieve those goals.

Saving for Education

According to www.canlearn.ca, by 2015, a child attending university away from home for four years will require approximately $150,000. A figure of that magnitude can give the most devoted parent a severe case of heartburn. But, before you reach for the antacids, remember that this money is actually an *investment* that you make in your child's future—and while the cost may be high, it is not unattainable.

Calculating Education Costs

There are various online calculators that can help you figure out what post-secondary education will cost, and how much you'll need to save. A very good general one (for basic information) and a more advanced one (with choices of specific institutions and provinces) are at www.canlearn.ca.

First of all, the cost of education can be reduced by about half if your child attends an institution in your own area and continues to live at home. And second, you should not expect to have to pay for your child's entire education yourself. He or she can and should be saving towards post-secondary education at least throughout the teen years, and can also be expected to work part-time and seasonally to help offset costs once attending college or university. Also, don't forget the availability of student loans, grants, bursaries, and scholarships.

The question still remains, of course, as to how you'll save the portion of funding that you *do* want to contribute.

Registered Education Savings Plans (RESPs)

RESPs are probably the most common way for people to save money towards their children's education. These are government-approved education savings plans that are offered by banks, credit unions, and other financial institutions and planners. Unlike RRSPs, contributions to an RESP are not tax deductible, so you'll still have to pay tax on whatever amount you deposit to the fund. The tax benefit comes later, when your child begins to withdraw funds for his or her continued education: While the interest that has accumulated is taxable, a student typically has little other income and so pays little or no tax on the RESP income.

SUCCESS TIP

An RESP cannot be used for all institutions or educational programs. Check with Human Resources Development Canada to make sure your choice qualifies.

Basic RESP Rules

- An RESP can be set up in the name of any child who has a social insurance number (SIN). Forms for obtaining SINs are available from Human Resources Development Canada.

- Anyone can open and contribute to an RESP for a child, but only the sponsor(s) of a particular plan can contribute to that plan.

- A combined total of $4,000 per year (from all sponsors) can be contributed to a child's RESP fund(s).

- Lifetime contributions on a child's behalf are limited to a total of $42,000 (from all sponsors combined).

- If contributions are returned to the sponsor (if a plan is collapsed), they are not taxed.

- RESP funds earn interest tax-free until the child is enrolled in a qualifying education program.

- The Canadian government provides a grant of up to $400 (20 per cent of the first $2,000) per year under the Canada Education Savings Grant (CESG).

- An RESP must be terminated by the end of its 26th year, so be sure that the funds are used up by that time.

A sponsor may contribute to an RESP for 22 years after it is opened.

If your child chooses not to continue his or her education in a qualifying program and you do not name a replacement beneficiary, you may be able to roll the funds over into your RRSP (or your spouse's) if the RESP has been in existence for at least 10 years, your child is 21 or older and not attending post-secondary education, and you're a Canadian citizen. If you have enough unused RRSP contribution room, there will be no penalty. If you do not have enough room, you will pay income tax at your marginal rate, plus a 20 per cent penalty tax over and above that marginal rate.

If you are contributing to RESPs on behalf of multiple children (who are related to each other and to you), you can set up a family plan. These plans are subject to the same contribution limits ($4,000 per year per beneficiary), but offer the advantage of being able to direct the entire income to only the child(ren) pursuing post-secondary education. For example, if you set up a family plan for your three children, and one chooses not to go on to a qualifying university, you can direct the RESP income to the two children who do continue their education.

A drawback to the family plan is that contributions are only allowed until the year that the youngest child turns 21 (an individual plan, on the other hand, allows you to contribute for 22 years after opening the RESP).

RESP Buyer Beware!

- An RESP is a contract between you and the plan provider. While RESPs are all government-approved, plans vary widely and may have more restrictions (on contributions, payouts, eligibility, etc.) than are legally required.

- RESPs can be invested in various funds, including aggressive-growth funds, which can make them vulnerable to poor performance or a potential loss of principal.

- "Scholarship trusts" are a type of plan that returns only the contributions to a subscriber if a child does not continue his/her education. Any investment income is retained to help fund other children who do continue.

- Watch out for hidden fees such as transaction fees, management fees, withdrawal fees, etc.

As with all funds, shop around and ask LOTS of questions!

Family Trusts

Another way to save for education is through a family trust. This is a legal way of holding property (including money) for the benefit of someone else (a beneficiary). The federal government has removed much of the incentive to create a family trust by taxing trust income received by minor beneficiaries at the top marginal tax rate, and by making parents responsible for paying that amount (the so-called "kiddie tax"), but beneficiaries can still take advantage of capital gains that are not included in this tax.

A trust is legally recognized as a separate person. As such, it pays tax separately and must file its own income tax return.

Even with taxation, simple payments out of the trust to a child aged 18 or older still make sense, because it is the child who will pay the tax (most likely at a lower rate because of his or her lower income).

SUCCESS TIPS

- Setting up a trust can be complicated, and will most likely require legal assistance and professional tax advice.

- Stay informed about future changes to tax laws, because the government could try to close the existing capital gains loophole in trust tax.

- Be aware that of the 21-year rule: Every 21 years, the proceeds of a trust must be distributed. If you're starting a trust for education purposes while your children are very young, this rule could work against your plans. Make sure you get professional advice!

Life Insurance

Life insurance can also be used as a savings vehicle for education needs. You can do this through a cash-value life insurance policy on your child's life, where part of the premium (which you pay) is invested for the child. When the child reaches 18, the policy is transferred to him/her on a tax-free (rollover) basis. There is no tax liability until the earnings are withdrawn by the child, at which time the child is taxed at his/her income level. The advantages to this method of saving include:

• Limitless investment (beyond insurability)

• Tax-deferred earnings

• Tax-free death benefit

• Guaranteed insurability for the insured child

• Contributions can be withdrawn tax-free from the cash value of the policy

• There are no restrictions on how the funds are used; if a child chooses not to go to university, for example, the funds could be used to purchase a house, start a business, or for travel

Of course, there are disadvantages as well. These include:

• Insurability: Some medical conditions will limit your child's insurability, and premiums will increase with age.

• It is generally an expensive method of saving.

• Life insurance plans are not registered as RESPs, therefore the Canada Education Savings Grant (CESG) does not apply.

• The penalty for cancellation in the first two years is significant.

• If you surrender the policy in order to get the cash value, the insurance is cancelled and you could trigger taxable capital gains.

Retiring Your Mortgage

A final education savings method is to retire your mortgage (pay it off) and then invest the money that you were putting toward your payments. If your mortgage payment is currently $900 per month, after you pay it off you could conceivably save $10,800 per year towards education. This method assumes, of course, that you have no other available money for savings, that you can pay off the mortgage quickly, and that you'll be employed and earning a satisfactory income at the time your children enter post-secondary education. Since your employment/health cannot be guaranteed, you should make sure that your life and disability insurance policies include a payout for your children's education, should you be unable to continue working in your later years.

Saving for Retirement

If you are depending on the Canada or Quebec Pension Plan (CPP or QPP) to fund your retirement, you could be in for a nasty surprise. First, there are many indications that, once the baby boomers hit full retirement age, both CPP and QPP will be seriously underfunded because the number of retirees drawing on the funds will greatly outnumber the workers still paying into them. And second, the maximum pensionable earnings for CPP, currently set by the government at about $38,000, will result in a much smaller payment than you might expect. At present, the highest possible CPP payment is $780 per month.

Calculate Your Needs

Want to know how much you'll need for your retirement income? The Canadian government provides a retirement income calculator on the Web at https://srv260.hrdc-drhc.gc.ca.

Also keep in mind that the amount you receive from CPP/QPP will depend on your age when you apply and the amount you've paid into the fund over the course of your working life. (If you haven't contributed at all, you won't qualify.)

Of course, CPP/QPP is not the only source of funding for aging Canadians. Old Age Security (OAS), the cornerstone of our retirement income system, is available to all Canadians aged 65 or older, regardless of income. Once your income exceeds $53,000, however, part of the OAS is "clawed back" at tax time. This clawback rises proportionally with your income until you end up losing the full amount when your net income hits about $80,000.

OAS is also proportional to the time you've lived in Canada. A Canadian who has spent at least 40 years in Canada after the age of 18 will receive the full amount of OAS. For someone who has lived here for less than 40 years, the amount of the pension will vary.

For pensioners who receive the OAS, but who have little or no other income, the Guaranteed Income Supplement (GIS) program is designed to provide additional funding. GIS is not taxable, but benefits are low and vary according to marital status and base income (a single pensioner receives about $500, and a married pensioner about $325).

Did You Know?

Neither OAS nor GIS are automatic—benefits must be applied for when you turn 65.

As you can see, even with the combined funds from CPP/QPP, OAS, and GIS, you will most likely be facing a drastically reduced income at a time when many of your expenses (due to age and declining health) could very well be increasing. To guard against this, you'll need another source of income, most easily achieved through planned retirement savings.

Registered Retirement Savings Plans (RRSPs)

While it is not the only approach to saving for retirement, the Registered Retirement Savings Plan, or RRSP, is probably the best-known vehicle for doing so. RRSPs offer significant tax advantages for most people: Contributions are tax-deductible, and any income earned in an RRSP isn't taxed until it's withdrawn (usually at retirement, when a reduced income puts you into a lower tax bracket). In addition, compounded interest (interest earned on interest) is not taxed at all, which effectively increases your "principal."

RRSP Contribution Limits

2003 - $14,500

2004 - $15,500

2005 - $16,500

2006 - $18,000

RRSPs are not without their disadvantages, however. The amount you can contribute to one is limited (calculated at 18 per cent of your income the previous year), and this can put a cap on how much money low- and middle-income earners are able to save for RRSPs. Any contributions in excess of your limit will be taxed as they earn income. If you're just starting out with an RRSP, you need expert advice. The rules and regulations are many, and to receive the full tax benefits, you need to follow them. As well, keep in mind these tips:

• Name beneficiaries of your RRSP so that if you die, the RRSP will not have to pass through your estate (making it subject to probate fees and in certain cases, income tax).

• Make sure your RRSP portfolio is diversified for maximum gain and minimum risk. Take full advantage of the foreign content rules (currently 30 per cent).

- Contribute to a spousal RRSP if your spouse is younger than you. This will maximize compounding by letting funds remain in place longer.

- Review your RRSP returns regularly to monitor their perform- ance. If you are using a financial advisor and you are concerned about some aspect of your portfolio's performance, speak to the advisor—don't let the concern fester.

RRSP Overcontributions

There is a zero penalty for up to $2,000 in overcontributions to an RRSP. Any amount over that is subject to a penalty of one per cent per month.

- Whenever possible, make the maximum annual contribution in order to get full compounding value and tax deductions.

- If you self-administer your RRSP, pay your fees personally, instead of through your holding company, self-employment business, or the plan itself. That way the fees will be tax deductible.

A Word Of Caution

If you decide to administer your own RRSP, make sure you know the rules! Not all assets qualify for RRSP holdings, and there are severe penalties if you hold non-qualifying ones.

- Consolidate your plans so that you're paying fewer fees and to make sure you're adhering to your foreign holdings allowance.

- Don't base your decision regarding an RRSP fund on administra- tion fees alone. If a low-fee fund isn't performing well, you'll lose money rather than save it.

• Don't wait until the RRSP deadline to contribute. Contribute as early in the year as possible, even if it's in small, monthly amounts. You'll increase the amount of your RRSP sooner, so that it grows faster, and it will be easier to fund in small increments than trying to scrape together a large lump sum at or near the deadline (or, even worse, having to get an RRSP loan in order to contribute).

Rule of 72

To calculate how long it will take to double your investment when you receive compound interest, divide 72 by the interest rate that you are receiving, e.g., $10,000 invested at six per cent will double in 12 years; at eight per cent it will double in nine years.

The sooner in your life that you can begin contributing to an RRSP, the faster your funds will grow. Remember that earnings on an RRSP are compounding, and every year you delay will cost you part of this compounding effect.

Contributions to an RRSP make the most sense for income earners whose marginal tax rate is over 50 per cent, because their income will most likely decrease after retirement, meaning that their marginal tax rate also decreases. In other words, they'll withdraw their RRSP funds at a lower tax rate, and their taxes on the fund's growth will also be paid at the lower rate.

But RRSPs are still extremely important for those of you in the middle marginal tax brackets, as well. They are one of the only tax deferral vehicles that can help you save for your retirement. Without them, you'll have to rely on government assistance, and possibly face a drastically reduced standard of living.

If you're in a low-income bracket, however, RRSPs can actually work *against* you (as unbelievable as this sounds!). While most Canadians' marginal tax rates decrease when they retire, the marginal tax rate for low-income earners actually *increases* (the actual marginal tax rate for a retiree is a minimum of 50 per cent. This is because for every dollar that a retiree's income increases (all RRSP withdrawals count as income), the GIS decreases by 50 cents. If you have to pay tax on that income as well, your combined tax rate could be 75 per cent. *And* the increase in income could also affect your eligibility for subsidized housing, prescription drug programs, and home and nursing care.

Borrowing for RRSPs

Be wary of borrowing to invest in an RRSP. Interest on funds that you borrow for RRSP contributions, unlike those for other investment purposes, are not tax-deductible. Remember that you can carry forward any unused contribution room, although doing so means you lose out on tax-deferred growth. A good rule of thumb is to borrow only if you can repay your RRSP loan within a year, and use your tax savings from the contribution to help pay down the loan.

Low-income Canadians are better advised to own their own homes. Most government income and asset-tested programs ignore a principal residence when determining eligibility, letting you take advantage of the equity you've built in your home without depriving you of income-tested benefits (see *Meeting the Shortfall* later in this chapter). In addition, investments in mutual funds, GICs, etc., also make sense. When these are cashed in, only the profit, and not the capital, will affect your eligibility for government asset- and income-tested programs.

Registered Retirement Income Funds (RRIFs)

If you do have RRSPs, you can contribute to them until you turn 69, after which, if you do nothing, you'll be taxed on the entire amount—definitely *not* a good thing for your financial waistline! The solution is a Registered Retirement Income Fund (RRIF), which provides a parking place for your RRSP funds and allows you to keep your principal intact while you pay tax only on the withdrawals that you make.

Investment rules for RRIFs are pretty much the same as they are for RRSPs, letting you continue to direct the fund as you see fit. However, because RRIFs are government-approved retirement income plans, there is a rule regarding withdrawals: A schedule requires an annually increasing percentage of payout, starting at about five per cent of assets when you're 70, and rising to 20 per cent by age 94 and older until you deplete your capital.

If you die, RRIFs, like RRSPs, will pass to your estate (and be subject to probate fees) unless you specify a beneficiary.

Annuities

An alternative to a RRIF is an annuity (if you use your RRSP funds to do this, it will be called an RRSP annuity). An annuity works like this: You give an insurer or financial institution a large lump sum, in exchange for which they'll pay you a set amount, usually monthly, for either a set term or the rest of your life.

Annuities do not provide any cash to your estate when you die. Instead, the annuity company will keep any balance remaining, unless there is a provision to continue payments to another person such as your spouse. However, if you die soon after making your annuity purchase, most companies have a guarantee period during which the annuity payments can be paid to a surviving spouse or other beneficiary.

Meeting the Shortfall

If, at retirement, you find yourself in a shortfall situation despite your best efforts (or perhaps your parents have found themselves in this situation), there are a number of possible remedies. First of all, if you are holding assets for your estate, consider leaving less or possibly nothing behind. Talk to your family about this decision so that if they're depending on an inheritance from you, they can make other arrangements and not be in for a big disappointment. You could also move in with one of your children, sell your home and purchase or rent something smaller, or look at a reverse mortgage.

Reverse Mortgages

A reverse mortgage is basically a type of annuity. If you own your home outright, you can mortgage the house for up to 35 per cent of its appraised value. The lender will purchase an annuity for you with the funds, which then provides a payment to you (you can take some of the proceeds as a lump sum).

> If the appraised value of your home is $250,000, the amount of your reverse mortgage would be $87,500 (35 per cent of $250,000).

While a reverse mortgage might sound like a good plan, there is a definite downside. During your lifetime, you make no mortgage payments; however, interest is still applied to the mortgage loan, and it compounds. If you die before the full value of your house is eaten up by this compounding interest, the house is sold and any equity goes to your estate. If you live longer than expected and the mortgage grows beyond the value of the house, the house is still sold, but your estate will receive nothing because there is no remaining equity (the annuity company absorbs the loss).

Another drawback—often not considered until it's too late—is the loss of a family home. Unless the family plans to buy the house back from the bank/annuity company at full market value, they no longer have any right to it.

Other Alternatives

There are alternatives to a straight reverse mortgage. A credit-line reverse mortgage (currently available through credit unions) allows you to draw on a line of credit instead of having to purchase an annuity. The added benefit to this is that you can keep the family home simply by paying off the credit line.

A second alternative, offered by some municipalities, is a tax-deferral program, which lets property taxes abate during a senior's life. The deferred taxes become a lien on the property that must be paid back when the property is sold. Check with your municipality to see if this option is available to you.

Private investor sale-leaseback is a third option. You sell your home to a private investor with a lease back to yourself for 20 to 30 years. The buyer gains the increased value in housing prices; you get cash and can remain in your home. If you choose this approach, ensure that a lawyer reviews the contract. You don't want to find yourself on the street if the house is resold and the new owners evict you before the leaseback period expires.

A Word About Investing

There are, of course, a multitude of ways to invest outside of RRSPs, RRIFs, RESPs, etc. If you're interested in pursuing these other investments, there are many excellent books that provide in-depth advice regarding investing strategies. Just remember to reduce your debt to manageable levels first, and then be sure to work any strategies into your new, financially healthy eating plan.

CHAPTER SUMMARY

- Guarding against dietary setbacks is a necessary task. Remember to consider these aspects of guarding against setbacks.
    - Estate planning
        - Wills
        - Powers of attorney
    - Life insurance
    - Disability insurance
    - Household insurance
- Planning for future financial health means saving for your children's education and your retirement.
    - Saving for education
        - RESPs
        - Family trusts
        - Life insurance savings
        - Retiring your mortgage
    - Saving for retirement
        - CPP/QPP
        - OAS
        - GIS
        - RRSPs
        - RRIFs
        - Annuities
        - Meeting the shortfall
            - Reverse mortgages
            - Other alternatives

Conclusion

My friend Herb has a poster on his wall at home that reads "The person who dies with the most toys wins."

The first time I saw the poster, I understood the message to be that life was all about consuming; about having more and more things. And that those things determine who you are and what your status is in society.

But that's not true. Our worth isn't about who our parents are, or what we have or own. It's about *who* we are; knowing that we are essentially decent, and that we're doing our best every day.

One day, I asked Herb what the poster meant to him. He told me it meant that people should enjoy life while they're still healthy and able to do so, because they can't enjoy it once they're gone. He said that his father always told him that if you see something that you like—a*nd you can afford it*—buy it and enjoy it. Herb's father was a smart man.

So go ahead. Have toys...and have fun. Just be sure that you can afford the things that you buy, because successful finances are about spending wisely instead of indiscriminately. Living on credit is not, and never will be, the answer. Learn, and teach your family, that paying cash (and using credit *wisely*) is the better way of managing your finances, and the better, more relaxed, and far more enjoyable way of living.

Appendix A

Monthly Income and Expense Statement

YOUR FAMILY'S MONTHLY INCOME	
Salary	Total
Commissions	
Bonuses	
Contract	
Tax credits	
Alimony/child support	
Interest/dividend income	
Investment income	
Rental income	
Pension income	
Other income	
TOTAL MONTHLY INCOME	

YOUR FAMILY'S MONTHLY EXPENSES	
Fixed Expenses	
Federal income tax, provincial income tax, CPP, EI (if deducted at source)	
Rent/mortgage	
Utilities: (if on a monthly budget plan)	
Electricity	
Heat	
Daycare services	
Cable TV/specialty channels	
Service contracts (cleaning/lawn/snow removal, etc.)	
Car loan payments	
Alimony/child support	
Periodic & Variable Expenses	
Taxes:	
Personal income tax (if not deducted at source)	
Municipal tax (if not included in mortgage payments)	
Water tax (if applicable)	
Utilities: (if not on a monthly budget plan)	
Electricity	
Heat	
Insurance:	
Home/tenant	
Automobile	
Life/disability	

Health	
Vehicle registration	
Driver's licence fees	
Loan/debt payments	
Car maintenance, repairs	
Gas/oil	
Parking	
Public transportation, taxis	
Groceries	
Dining out	
Dry cleaning	
Clothing	
Babysitting	
Home maintenance/repairs	
Telephone (including long distance and cellular)	
Furniture	
Health:	
Medical, prescriptions	
Dental	
Recreation:	
Newspapers, magazines, books, videos	
Alcohol, beer, wine	
Movies, concerts, plays, etc.	
Recreational/club/court fees	
Pets:	
Pet food	

Veterinary bills	
Personal:	
Personal care items	
Hairdressing	
Tuition	
Charitable donations	
Gifts	
Vacations	
Miscellaneous	
Savings	
(a) Registered retirement savings	
(b) Non-registered savings	
(c) Registered education savings	
(d) Other	
TOTAL MONTHLY EXPENSES	$
Total Monthly Income:	
Total Monthly Expenses: −	
CASH REMAINING =	$

Appendix B

Calculating Your Family's Net Worth

FAMILY NET WORTH			
ASSETS	**You**	**Spouse/ Partner**	**Total**
Possessions			
House			
Furniture			
Antiques			
Artwork			
Collectibles			
Cottage			
Car(s)			
Other			
Investments & Savings			
Stocks			
Bonds			
RESPs			

	You	Spouse/Partner	Total
Mutual funds			
Cash value of life insurance			
Savings/chequing accounts			
Treasury bills			
Canada/provincial savings bonds			
GICs, term deposits			
Other investments			
Retirement Savings			
RRSPs			
Pension plans			
Deferred profit sharing plans			
Total Assets			
LIABILITIES			
Personal Debts			
Mortgage(s) on home			
Other mortgages			
Car loan(s)			
Line(s) of credit			
Credit card balances			
Other loans			
Unpaid bills			
Outstanding taxes			
Other			
Total Liabilities			
NEW WORTH	**You**	**Spouse/ Partner**	**Total**
Assets	$	$	$
Liabilities −			
YOUR FAMILY'S NET WORTH =	$	$	$

Appendix C

Credit Counselling Agencies in Canada

Alberta

Credit Counselling Services of Alberta
Calgary: (403) 265-2201
Edmonton: (780) 423-5265
Toll Free: 1-888-294-0076
info@creditcounselling.com

British Columbia

Credit Counselling Society of British Columbia
Vancouver: (604) 527-8999
Toll Free: 1-888-527-8999
info@nomoredebts.org

Manitoba

Community Financial Counselling Services
Winnipeg: (204) 989-1900
cfcs@mts.net

New Brunswick

Credit Counselling Services of Atlantic Canada, Inc.
Fredericton: (506) 450-4093
Moncton: (506) 382-5966
Saint John: (506) 652-1613
Toll Free: 1-888-753-2227
ccsinfo@ccsac.com

Newfoundland and Labrador

Credit Counselling Service of Newfoundland & Labrador
St. John's: (709) 753-5812
info@debthelpnewfoundland.com

Nova Scotia

Credit Counselling Services of Atlantic Canada, Inc.
Toll Free: 1-888-753-2227
Halifax: (902) 423-3236
Kentville: (902) 678-7552
csinfo@ccsac.com

Ontario

Barrie
Credit Counselling Service of Simcoe-Georgian Bay Region
(705) 726-2705

Belleville
Quinte Region Credit Counselling Service
(613) 966-3556

Brampton
Family Services of Peel
(905) 453-7890

Brantford
Family Counselling Centre of Brant, Inc.
(519) 753-4173

Brockville
1000 Islands Credit Counselling Service
(613) 498-2111
Brockville Credit Counselling
Toll Free: 1-800-379-5556

Cambridge
Catholic Family Counselling Centre
(519) 743-6333

Chatham
Family Service Kent
(519) 354-6221

Clinton
Family Services Perth-Huron
(519) 273-1020
Toll Free: 1-800-268-0903

Cornwall
Family Counselling Centre of Cornwall & United Counties
(613) 932-1266

Exeter
Family Services Perth-Huron
(519) 273-1020
Toll Free: 1-800-268-0903

Guelph
Family Counselling and Support Services for Guelph-Wellington
(519) 824-2431

Hamilton
Family Services, Hamilton
(905) 527-3823

Kingston
Kingston Community Counselling Centre
(613) 549-7850
Toll Free: 1-800-379-5556

Kitchener
Catholic Family Counselling Centre (Region of Waterloo)
(519) 743-6333

London
Credit Counselling London
(519) 433-0159

Markham
Markham Stouffville Family Life Centre
(905) 415-9719
Toll Free: 1-866-415-9723

Mississauga
Family Services of Peel
(905) 270-2235

North Bay
Community Counselling Centre of Nipissing
(705) 472-6515

Oakville
Halton Consumer Credit Counselling Service
(905) 842-1459

Oshawa
Credit Counselling Service of Durham Region
(905) 579-1951

Ottawa
Credit Counselling Service of Eastern Ontario
(613) 728-2041
Toll Free: 1-866-202-0425

Owen Sound
Family Services Perth-Huron
(519) 273-1020
Toll Free: 1-800-268-0903

Peterborough
Family Counselling Service of Peterborough
(705) 742-1351
Toll Free: 1-800-274-1611

Richmond Hill
Family and Credit Counselling Services
(905) 884-9148

Sarnia
Credit Counselling Services of Southwestern Ontario, Inc.
(519) 337-8757

Sault Ste. Marie
Credit Counselling Service of Sault Ste. Marie
(705) 254-1424

St. Catherines
Credit Counselling of Regional Niagara
(905) 684-9401
Toll Free: 1-800-663-3973

Stratford
Family Services Perth-Huron
(519) 273-1020
Toll Free: 1-800-268-0903

Sudbury
Sudbury Community Service Centre
(705) 560-0430
Toll Free: 1-800-685-1521

Thunder Bay
Family Services Thunder Bay
(807) 684-1880

Timmins
Credit Counselling Services of Cochrane District
(705) 267-5817

Toronto
Credit Counselling Service of Toronto
(416) 228-3328
Toll Free: 1-800-267-2272

Unionville
Markham Stouffville Family Life Centre
(905) 415-9719
Toll Free: 1-866-415-9723

Waterloo
Catholic Family Counselling Centre
(519) 743-6333

Windsor
Credit Counselling Services of Southwestern Ontario Inc.
(519) 258-2030

Prince Edward Island

Credit Counselling Services of PEI
(902) 892-2441
Toll Free: 1-866-892-2441

Quebec – contact either

Credit Counselling Services of Atlantic Canada
Toll Free: 1-866-753-2227

Credit Counselling Service of Eastern Ontario
Toll Free: 1-888-294-0076

Saskatchewan

Department of Justice, Provincial Mediation Board
Regina: (306) 787-5387
Saskatoon: (306) 933-6520
Toll Free: 1-888-215-2222

Regina
(306) 787-5387

Saskatoon
(306) 933-6520

Territories – contact either
Credit Counselling Services of Alberta
Toll Free: 1-888-294-0076

Credit Counselling Society of British Columbia
Toll Free: 1-888-527-8999

source: www.creditcounsellingcanada.ca

Appendix D

Provincial Consumer Protection Agencies

Alberta

Alberta Government Services
Consumer Services Branch
Floor 3, 10155-102 Street
Edmonton AB T5J 4L4
Tel.: (780) 427-4088
Toll Free (in Alberta): 1-877-427-4088
Fax: (780) 422-9106
Email: consumer.services@gov.ab.ca
Web Site: www.gov.ab.ca/gs

Room 301, 7015 Macleod Trail South
Calgary AB T2H 2K6
Tel.: 1-877-427-4088
Fax: (403) 297-4270

British Columbia

Ministry of Attorney General
Community Justice Branch
Consumer Services Division
Consumer Services Head Office
5th Floor, 1019 Wharf Street
Victoria BC V8V 1X4

Mailing Address
PO Box 9297, Station Prov Govt
Victoria BC V8W 9J8
Tel.: (250) 387-3045
Fax: (250) 953-3533
Email: consumer@ag.gov.bc.ca
Web Site: www.pssg.gov.bc.ca/consumers

Investigations/Trade Practices

Motor Dealer Licensing: (250) 387-5433

Cemetery and Funeral Services: (250) 387-1271

Debt Collection: (250) 387-1627

Regional Offices
Suite 402, 4211 Kingsway
Burnaby BC V5H 1Z6
Tel.: (604) 660-3570
Fax: (604) 660-3521

Investigations/Trade Practices
Travel/Direct Sellers: (604) 660-3540
100 Cranbrook Street N.
Cranbrook BC V1C 3P9
Tel.: (250) 426-1497
Fax: (250) 426-1561

235-1st Avenue
Kamloops BC V2C 3J4
Tel.: (250) 828-4667
Fax: (250) 371-3822

1726 Dolphin Avenue
Kelowna BC V1Y 9R9
Tel.: (250) 717-2019
Fax: (250) 717-2021

1044-5th Avenue
Prince George BC V2L 5M2
Tel.: (250) 565-6030
Fax: (250) 565-6180

Manitoba

Consumers Bureau
Manitoba Consumer and Corporate Affairs
302-258 Portage Avenue
Winnipeg MB R3C 0B6
Tel.: (204) 945-3800
Toll Free: 1-800-782-0067
Fax: (204) 945-0728
Email: consumersbureau@cca.gov.mb.ca
Web Site: www.gov.mb.ca/cca/consumb

New Brunswick

Consumer Affairs Branch
Department of Justice
670 King Street
PO Box 6000
Fredericton NB E3B 5H1
Tel.: (506) 462-5100
Fax: (506) 453-7483
Email: al@gov.nb.ca
Web Site: www.gov.nb.ca/justice

Newfoundland and Labrador

Consumer Affairs
Department of Government Services and Lands
2nd Floor, Confederation Building West Block
PO Box 8700
St. John's NF A1B 4J6
Tel.: (709) 729-2600
Fax: (709) 729-3205
Web Site: www.gov.nf.ca/gsl/cca/tpl/default.stm

Northwest Territories

Consumer Services
Community Operations Programs
Municipal and Community Affairs
Room 500, 5201-50th Avenue
Yellowknife NWT X1A 3S9
Tel.: (867) 873-7125
Fax: (867) 920-6343
Email: mgagnon@maca.gov.nt.ca
Web Site: www.maca.gov.nt.ca

Nova Scotia

Service Nova Scotia and Municipal Relations
PO Box 2502
Halifax NS B3J 3N5
Tel.: (902) 424-5200
Toll Free: 1-800-670-4357
Fax: (902) 424-0720
Web Site: www.gov.ns.ca/snsmr

Nunavut

Consumer Affairs
Community Government and Transportation
PO Box 440

Baker Lake NU X0C 0A0
Tel.: (867) 793-3303
Toll Free: 1-866-456-2304
Fax: (867) 793-3321

Ontario

Ministry of Consumer and Business Services
General Inquiry Unit
35th Floor, 250 Yonge Street
Toronto ON M5B 2N5
Tel.: (416) 326-8555
Toll Free: 1-800-268-1142
Web Site: www.cbs.gov.on.ca

Prince Edward Island

Consumer, Corporate and Insurance Services
Office of the Attorney General
4th Floor, 95 Rochford Street
PO Box 2000
Charlottetown PEI C1A 7N8
Tel.: (902) 368-4580
Toll Free: 1-800-658-1799
Fax: (902) 368-5283
Web Site: www.gov.pe.ca

Quebec

Office de la protection du consommateur
Room 450, 400 Jean-Lesage Boulevard
Québec QC G1K 8W4
Tel.: 1-888-672-2556
Web Site: www.opc.gouv.qc.ca

Saskatchewan

Consumer Protection Branch
Saskatchewan Department of Justice
1871 Smith Street
Regina SK S4P 3V7
Tel.: (306) 787-5550
Toll Free (in Saskatchewan): 1-888-374-4636
Fax: (306) 787-9779
Email: consumerprotection@justice.gov.sk.ca

Yukon

Department of Justice
Consumer Services Branch
PO Box 2703
Whitehorse YK Y1A 2C6
Tel.: (867) 667-5111
Toll Free: 1-800-661-0408
Fax: (867) 667-3609
Email: consumers@gov.yk.ca

The Andrew Philipson Law Centre
2130-2nd Avenue
Whitehorse YK Y1A 5C3
Tel.: (867) 667-5111

source: http://strategis.ic.gc.ca/SSG/ca01506e.html#c

Appendix E

Summary of Intestacy Laws in Canada

Province	Preferential Share	Spouse + 1 Child	Spouse + 2 Children	No Spouse, 1 Child	No Spouse, 2 Children	No Spouse, No Children No Parents
		Remaining Assets				
Alberta	$40,000	1/2 to spouse / 1/2 to child	1/3 to spouse / 1/3 to each child	All provinces and territories: all to child	All provinces and territories: children share equally	All provinces and territories except Quebec: parents share equally. Quebec: 1/2 to parents 1/2 to siblings. — All provinces and territories except Quebec: all to brothers and sisters. If no brothers or sisters alive, then to nieces and nephews equally. If no distant family, estate goes to provincial government. Quebec: brothers, sisters, nieces, and nephews share equally. If no brothers or sisters are living, then nieces and nephews share residue equally. If no next of kin can be found, estate goes to the government.
British Columbia	$65,000	1/2 to spouse / 1/2 to child	1/3 to spouse / 1/3 to each child			
Manitoba	$50,000	All to spouse	All to spouse			
New Brunswick	Nil	1/2 to spouse / 1/2 to child	1/3 to spouse / 1/3 to each child			
Newfoundland	Nil	1/2 to spouse / 1/2 to child	1/3 to spouse / 1/3 to each child			
Northwest Territories	$50,000	1/2 to spouse / 1/2 to child	1/3 to spouse / 1/3 to each child			
Nova Scotia	$50,000	1/2 to spouse / 1/2 to child	1/3 to spouse / 1/3 to each child			
Nunavut	$50,000	1/2 to spouse / 1/2 to child	1/3 to spouse / 1/3 to each child			
Ontario	$200,000	1/2 to spouse / 1/2 to child	1/3 to spouse / 1/3 to each child			
Prince Edward Island	$50,000	1/2 to spouse / 1/2 to child	1/3 to spouse / 1/3 to each child			
Quebec	Nil	1/3 to spouse / 2/3 to child	1/3 to spouse / 1/3 to each child			
Saskatchewan	$100,000	1/2 to spouse / 1/2 to child	1/3 to spouse / 1/3 to each child			
Yukon	Nil	1/2 to spouse / 1/2 to child	1/3 to spouse / 1/3 to each child			

Glossary

Administrator under the *Bankruptcy and Insolvency Act* A person licenced by the Office of the Superintendent of Bankruptcy to file a Consumer Proposal or a Division I Commercial Proposal on behalf of either an individual or a company.

Alimony Money paid to an ex-spouse due to a court judgment.

Amortization The process of gradually paying down debt or obligation, e.g., a mortgage. For most individuals, amortization refers to the period of time over which payments will be made in order to pay a mortgage in full. Note that amortization is not the same as the term of a mortgage.

Annuity A contract with an insurance company that provides you with a series of payments in exchange for a lump-sum investment.

Appraised Value An estimate of the potential selling price of an asset, e.g., real estate.

APR Annual percentage rate on a loan. Check the APR numbers to compare various loan offers.

Arrears   Money that is overdue and unpaid. The term usually applies to support payments and mortgages.

Assignment in Bankruptcy   A document transferring an insolvent person's assets to a trustee in bankruptcy for the general benefit of his or her creditors.

Bankrupt   A person who has filed an assignment in bankruptcy with a bankruptcy trustee under Canada's *Bankruptcy and Insolvency Act*.

Bankruptcy   A formal proceeding under Canada's *Bankruptcy and Insolvency Act* that is available to an insolvent person who owes at least $1,000 and is unable to pay his or her debts as they come due.

Bankruptcy Estate   The assets owned by the trustee in bankruptcy after a person has gone bankrupt

Beneficiary   The person or organization who receives a monetary or property bequest in a will, trust, or investment.

Budget   A plan that allows you to allocate your financial resources where they can be best used.

Canada Education Savings Grant (CESG)   A grant given by the Canadian government to add to a person's education savings contributions.

Canada Pension Plan (CPP)   A Canadian government program funded by the premiums it collects, mainly through paycheque deductions. Every person who works must pay into the Canada Pension Plan and will receive a monthly payment upon retirement.

Child Support   Money paid from one parent to another for the benefit of the child.

Collateral   An asset of value that is pledged against a loan in case of default. If default occurs, the lender can use the asset to pay down the loan.

Collection Agency   A business that attempts to collect a debt that the original creditor has deemed uncollectable.

Community Property (or Family Property)   A legal term that describes assets acquired during the marriage that are jointly shared by both parties.

Consumer Credit   Credit used by individuals and families for personal needs, including mortgages, personal, business, and agricultural loans.

Consumer Proposal   When making a consumer proposal, individuals usually offer creditors a percentage of what they owe over a specified period of time (not exceeding five years). This is a formal proceeding under Canada's *Bankruptcy and Insolvency Act* that is available to a debtor whose total debts do not exceed $75,000 (excluding any mortgages on the personal residence). If a husband and wife make a proposal, the total debts cannot exceed $150,000 (excluding any mortgages on their personal residence).

Credit   An agreement under which a person borrows money to purchase an asset or service.

Credit Cards   Used by consumers to charge purchases to their account. Users are required to make a minimum monthly payment every month.

Credit Counselling   Advice from a trained professional on reducing debt through various proven means.

Credit Limit   The maximum amount that you can charge to a credit card or the maximum amount that you can borrow.

Credit Rating   A record of an individual's credit worthiness and payment history. Various credit bureaus maintain and update such records, providing this information to financial institutions and other businesses.

Credit Report   The report that details your credit history and bill-paying habits.

Debt   A form of indebtedness owed by a person to a lender, whether it be by way of a loan, line of credit, or other type of debt instrument.

Debtor   A person who receives a loan or an advance of goods or service in exchange for a promise to repay at a later date.

Default   The failure to make payments on a mortgage, line of credit, credit card, loan, or other debt.

Discharge from Bankruptcy   A bankruptcy court order releasing a person from his or her legal obligation to repay debts. To receive a discharge, a person must have complied with his or her duties under the *Bankruptcy and Insolvency Act* and cooperated with the trustee. Depending on circumstances, discharge can be absolute, conditional on other obligations being fulfilled, or suspended for a specified length of time.

Equity   The difference between the value of an asset and what is owed against that asset.

Estate Administrator (formerly known as an administrator /administratrix)   A person or institution who administers the estate of a deceased person and is appointed by the court. If someone dies without a will, or a will fails to name an estate trustee, the estate administrator handles the duties of overseeing the estate.

Estate Planning   The planning required, usually with the help of financial and legal advisors, to preserve wealth for family and future generations. It involves planning tools and techniques that can reduce estate taxes and make a smooth transition for your affairs after your death.

Estate Trustee (formerly known as an executor/executrix)   A person or institution who is named in the will to administer the estate of a deceased person, and is appointed by the court to handle the duties set out in the will.

Family Property *See* "Community Property."

First Meeting of Creditors A meeting that, if called by the creditors, the bankrupt must attend. During this meeting, the debtor will be questioned about his assets and debts.

Garnishment The legal proceeding by a creditor to seize a debtor's bank accounts, wages, or other monies.

Grace Period Time available after the credit card statement date in which the borrower can pay off the outstanding balance without any further interest charges being added to the account (the "payment due" date). Bank credit cards usually have a grace period of 15 to 21 days. Retail credit cards usually have a 30-day grace period. No grace period applies to cash advances because interest begins immediately.

Guardian A person who has been legally designated to care for the needs of a minor child or other individual who is incapable of managing his or her own affairs.

Home Equity Loan (or Line of Credit) A home loan that provides the debtor with a loan amount equal to the equity in his property and sometimes even more.

Insolvent The state of not being able to meet your financial obligations.

Interest The cost of borrowing money, or when you deposit money into a bank, the bank pays you money on the deposit.

Intestate A person who dies without leaving a valid will.

Introductory Rate (or Teaser Rate) An interest rate, often a very low one, offered to entice you to choose one credit card over another.

Joint Tenants Two or more people who jointly own real estate or stocks and bonds. If one joint tenant dies, his or her share automatically belongs to the other joint tenant(s), regardless of what a will says (except in Quebec).

Judgment   The formal decision or court order deciding a lawsuit and setting out the amount of a creditor's claim against a debtor. This constitutes final legal proof that a creditor's claim against a debtor is proper and permits the creditor to continue with further legal action to collect its debt, such as garnishment or a lien against the debtor's property.

Lien   A claim upon property used to secure payment of a debt. After the debt is paid, the lien is removed.

Line of Credit   *See* "Home Equity Loan."

Minimum Payment   The least you must pay to avoid any other fees. Paying the minimum will ensure that, over the course of the repayment period, you will pay the maximum.

Mortgage   A promise to repay a debt, together with interest, at a certain interest rate over a specific period of time. Usually registered against real estate or personal property.

Net Worth   Total assets less total liabilities.

Overdraft Protection   Protection allowed to consumers to overdraw their chequing account up to a specified limit. Interest is charged only on the overdrawn amount every month. The interest rate is usually much higher than current loan rates.

Overspending   Going into debt by spending more money than you have. Often, compulsive overspending is treated as an addiction.

Personal Property   All property that you own other than real estate.

Principal   The amount you actually borrow. If you charge a $300 plane ticket, that is your principal.

Proposal   An alternative to bankruptcy, whereby a trustee and the insolvent come up with a repayment plan to the satisfaction of the creditors.

Registered Education Savings Plan (RESP) A registered savings and investment plan that accumulates funds in a tax-sheltered environment in order to pay for post-secondary education. Contributions made to an RESP are not deductible from taxable income. The plan is terminated if the funds are not used for post-secondary educational purposes.

Registered Retirement Income Fund (RRIF) Once the owner of an RRSP reaches a certain age (now 69), the money must be converted from an RRSP to a RRIF. The RRIF requires that the owner withdraw a specified minimum amount every year.

Registered Retirement Savings Plan (RRSP) A savings plan that also acts as a tax-deferral plan to encourage Canadians to save for their retirement. RRSPs allow the owner to defer the payment of income tax on the income invested in the RRSP until the funds are withdrawn or transferred to an RRIF.

Repossession The action taken by the creditor to reclaim property after a debtor defaults on a loan to purchase the property.

Reverse Mortgage A mortgage against a home that is used to purchase an annuity that provides a monthly income to the homeowner. Usually purchased by elderly people who need to supplement low monthly incomes.

Sue To commence a legal proceeding intended to recover monetary damages.

Superintendent of Bankruptcy An official appointed by the Canadian government to oversee the administration of Canada's *Bankruptcy and Insolvency Act*.

Surplus Income Payments When people declare bankruptcy, they are no longer required to make payments to creditors. However, as long as they remain undischarged, they may be expected to pay to their Trustee in Bankruptcy a portion of any income that exceeds reasonable living expenses. These payments are based on guidelines issued yearly by the Superintendent of Bankruptcy. If a bankrupt has surplus income and fails to make voluntary payments to the Trustee, the court may order such payment or delay the discharge from bankruptcy.

Tax Credits   Credits for GST rebates, etc., that may be available to someone filing an income tax return.

Teaser Rate   *See* "Introductory Rate."

Term Insurance   A life insurance policy that covers a person for a stated term, e.g., five or 10 years. After the policy reaches its term, the insurance policy is automatically terminated.

Transaction Fees   Fees charged for each use of a credit card or bank account (for withdrawals, transfers, point-of-sale purchases, etc.).

Trustee in Bankruptcy   A person licenced by the Office of the Superintendent of Bankruptcy to file a bankruptcy on behalf of either an individual or a company.

Universal Life   A form of whole life insurance that provides life insurance coverage, as well as an insurance component indexed to money market funds. Universal life's popularity is greatest when interest rates are high.

Variable Life   A form of whole life insurance in which the investment portion of the plan is invested in mutual funds. These plans are more flexible and potentially provide higher returns than universal policies; they are not, however, as predictable.

Frequently
Asked Questions

1. COLLECTION AGENCIES

Q: I am being harassed by a collection agency to collect money that
I don't owe. They call me at the office, speak to my co-workers and
my boss, and threaten them and me. My family and I get calls at
home during the day, in the evening, and on weekends. What can I
do to stop this harassment?

A: A collection agency is an organization that either obtains payment or arranges for payment of monies owed to their client. I
assume that you have told the collection agency that you do not owe
the debt and that they are persisting in their attempts to collect it.

In Ontario and in other provinces, the *Collection Agencies Act* sets
out a code of ethics by which collection agencies and collectors
must abide. The following are some things that collection agencies
cannot do:

- Try to collect a debt without first notifying the debtor in writing,
  at the debtor's last known address, that the collection agency has
  the account assigned to it

- Recommend or initiate legal action on the collection of a debt without first notifying the debtor and obtaining the creditor's written permission

- Make telephone and personal calls of such a nature or frequency to constitute harassment of the debtor or the debtor's family

- Call to collect a debt on a Sunday, a statutory holiday, or before 7:00 a.m. or after 9:00 p.m.

- Imply or give out false or misleading information that could damage the debtor or the debtor's family

- Demand payment of the debt without giving the name and authority of the creditor and the collector, and the balance of the money owed

- Continue to collect payment from a person who claims not to owe the money, unless the collector has tried every way to ensure that the person actually is the debtor

In addition, collectors are generally not allowed to contact the debtor's friends, employer, relatives, or neighbours other than to obtain the debtor's phone number or address. The only exception is contacting a person about a debt that he or she has guaranteed to pay for the debtor, or contacting an employer about payment connected to a wage assignment or court order, or to confirm employment.

In Ontario, collection agencies and collectors are regulated by the Ministry of Consumer and Business Services. If you feel that any regulations have been breached by the collection agency or the collector, contact the head of the collection agency. If this doesn't solve the problem, you can contact the Ministry at (416) 326-9768 or 1-800-889-9768 to file a complaint. You can even file a complaint online at www.cbs.gov.on.ca/mcbs/english/2452_3fe.htm.

A list of other agencies throughout Canada is located in Appendix "D".

2. NON-FILING OF INCOME TAX RETURNS

Q: I haven't filed a personal income tax return for several years. Should I contact Revenue Canada myself or wait until they find me? What will happen to me?

A: Revenue Canada has become the Canada Customs and Revenue Agency (CCRA), and, yes, you need to contact them as soon as possible. If you think you may be assessed penalties over and above any interest on money you owe, seek the help of their Voluntary Disclosures Program. This allows individuals to provide tax or customs information that was either not reported or misreported in previous years, without penalty. It also allows you to anonymously seek advice and information that will help you prepare for submitting your paperwork for voluntary disclosure.

If you make a voluntary disclosure before the CCRA begins an audit, investigation, or other action, you will only have to pay what you owe, plus interest; they will not prosecute or impose any other penalties. Your disclosure must meet four conditions: it must be initiated by you (without you knowing about an upcoming audit or investigation); it must be complete and accurate; it must involve a monetary penalty; and it must involve information one or more years overdue.

Of course, if your situation doesn't involve a penalty, you'll still need to file prior year adjustments and pay any amounts owing to bring your file up to date.

The CCRA recognizes that sometimes extraordinary circumstances, such as serious illness or natural disasters, prevent Canadians from complying with income tax laws. In these cases, they have some discretion to cancel, reduce, or waive interest and penalties under their fairness provisions.

To make a voluntary disclosure or to get more information, contact the CCRA at 1-800-959-8281 or log onto their Web site at www.ccra-adrc.gc.ca.

3. RE-ESTABLISHING CREDIT

Q: I'm trying to re-establish a good credit rating, and I've heard about a secured credit card. What exactly is it, and is it a good idea?

A: A secured credit card works the same way as any other, but it's secured by money that you deposit with the credit card's issuer. In most cases, your credit limit is equal to the deposit. You'll earn interest on the money you've deposited, but if you don't make the required payments on your credit purchases, the credit card issuer can use the deposit to pay what you owe.

There is usually a monthly fee for the card, and the interest rate may be somewhat higher than average. Also, if the account goes into arrears, an extra fee or higher interest could be charged.

Is it a good idea? That depends on you. If you're able to meet the terms of the agreement and have taken steps to correct former poor credit habits, it can certainly help you restore your credit standing.

Talk to your personal banking advisor at your financial institution to see if they can offer you this option. The Home Trust Company also offers a secured VISA card (1-877-569-6333; www.hometrust.ca).

4. BANKRUPTCY AND THE FAMILY HOME

Q: After my ex-husband and I separated, I was awarded exclusive possession of our jointly owned matrimonial home. He then declared bankruptcy, and now the bankruptcy firm wants me to pay them for his share of the home. I've ignored them so far, because I can't afford a lawyer. I don't believe I should have to pay for his bankruptcy, and I think they're asking for an excessive amount. What should I do?

A: While you were given exclusive possession of the matrimonial home, you were not given exclusive ownership of it. The ownership remained in both your name and your husband's. When your husband declared bankruptcy, the trustee in bankruptcy became the owner of his share of the property, subject to its outstanding mortgages.

The trustee either wants you to buy out the trustee's share in the property (which used to be your husband's share), or have the property sold and the net equity (what's left after the mortgage is paid out) divided between the trustee and yourself.

You should consider having a certified appraiser, registered with the Appraisal Institute of Canada, determine the value of the property at the time of your husband's bankruptcy. This will give you an independent opinion of its worth. Then hire a lawyer specializing in bankruptcy to negotiate your purchase of the trustee's share.

If you choose to do nothing, the trustee will apply for the partition and sale of your house, which may force you to leave your home. You are much better off if you can agree upon an amount with the trustee, and then pay the trustee that amount of money over a period of time. You may also be able to negotiate a payment plan with the lawyer to make the process more affordable.

5. PREPAID (SECURED) CREDIT CARDS

Q: My teen read about prepaid credit cards in one of her U.S.-based magazines. What do I tell her?

A: What your teen probably read about is a card called Visa Buxx. It's currently available only in the U.S., but the concept is receiving attention here at home. Visa Buxx isn't an actual credit card, but what's called a stored value card.

It works like this: You, the parent, open the card for your teen by loading an amount of cash onto the card. You're the only one who can add money to the card, and your teen has access only to that amount. The card can be used anywhere Visa is accepted, and is processed by merchants in the same manner as a credit card. While the card is not intended to carry a negative balance, you need to be aware that if a merchant puts through a purchase without prior authorization, a negative balance is possible. This in turn could result in a penalty fee.

The card is being touted as a budgeting tool in that you can control your teen's spending and monitor the balances and purchases being made (via Web site or phone), perhaps opening up discussions between you and your teen on the topic of money management.

While it is certainly safer to carry than cash (and may be more convenient while on vacation, etc.) your teen might not be entirely amenable to having you look over her shoulder in this manner. If these cards become available in Canada, you'll want to discuss the pros and cons with her carefully.

6. MORTGAGING YOUR HOUSE TO PLAY THE STOCK MARKET

Q: I'd like to invest in the stock market, and my neighbour suggested mortgaging my house to get the funds I need. Is this wise?

A: You need to think this through carefully. It's called home-equity leverage, and as tempting as it is to rush out to the bank during a rising market, the strategy is extremely risky. If you have long-term goals and a strong stomach, it might be an option for you—if you can also afford to lose your home. The stock market is volatile, and you need to consider how it would affect you if the bottom dropped out of the market tomorrow.

Some of the biggest problems in leveraging are for people in their 50s or 60s. While they might have built up considerable equity in their homes, they don't have the time to wait out the market if it takes a downturn. They may need to access their retirement investment before it has regained its value.

Other investors need to tread cautiously, too. You might be able to increase your leverage to huge levels with a home equity loan, but your risk increases just as much. Make the wrong investments, lose the money, default on your payments, and the bank gets your house.

If your neighbour's reasoning is that property values are relatively stable and that leveraging your equity lets you put your money into a more suitable investment vehicle, remember that it's not your neighbour's house that they're suggesting you put at risk.

Bottom line? Decide if you could afford to lose your home, and think about getting a second opinion.

7. GAMBLING ADDICTIONS

Q: My husband likes to gamble so much that I think he may have a problem. Recently I've been getting calls from some of our creditors about overdue payments for bills he told me were paid. We have two children and I'm worried about our finances. What can I do?

A: A gambling problem can result in serious financial trouble, and you need to talk to your husband about what's happening. If it's clear that his gambling is the source of the problem, send a letter immediately to your bank telling them you'll honour what's due to this point on any joint lines of credit, but not beyond. Do the same for any joint credit cards (both bank and retail), and ask to have your name removed from the cards. If a credit card is in your name with your husband listed only as co-cardholder, have his name removed and tell the creditor you won't honour any more of his charges.

Stop making deposits to any joint accounts, and open accounts in your name only. If your husband controls any trust accounts for your children, try to have him agree to changing the name over to yours. If he's uncooperative, you may need to seek legal help.

Regardless of whether major assets (house, car, etc.) are in his name only, or you are jointly responsible for mortgages and loans, credit counselling is essential. Call the credit counselling services listed on Appendix "C" of this book.

You should also contact Gamblers Anonymous at www.gamblersanonymous.org.

8. CREDIT REPAIR

Q: My credit record has been a little shaky over the last few years. A friend told me about an advertisement he saw for a company offering to clean up your credit rating for you. Is this legitimate?

A: Possibly not. Some credit repair clinics claim to be able to remove negative information (including bankruptcies and default judgments) from your credit records for a fee. They can't. Credit bureaus get their information about you from the places that have given you credit, such as banks and credit card companies, and the courts. Their obligation is to keep your credit record complete and current. If the record is accurate, no one can make them change it.

Some clinics simply obtain your credit record, check for errors, and help you correct them, but you don't need to pay for this; you can do it yourself for free. Request your credit record from the bureau holding your file (check your Yellow Pages under Credit Reporting Agencies). If you can prove it contains errors or incomplete information, ask in writing to have it corrected. The agency then has to inform anyone you say has received the old information in the past six to 12 months.

If there's a bankruptcy or proposal involved, be patient. A bankruptcy stays on your credit record for at least six years after discharge; a proposal stays for three years after completion.

Once your credit record is accurate, begin re-establishing your credit rating by cautious use of credit, and making all of your payments on time. It's slow, but it works.

9. CREDIT COUNSELLING

Q: I have credit card debts that I can't pay, my bank account is overdrawn, and I can't make my mortgage payments. When I seek credit counselling, should I mention that I have two cars? Should I declare bankruptcy, and if I do, can I keep the cars?

A: You're right to take action, and should do so as quickly as possible. Credit counselling services available across Canada can set up a debt management program for you with your creditors. (And, yes, you must declare both cars.) See Appendix "C" for a provincial listing of these agencies.

Consolidating your debts may help. Ask your financial institution if you can combine all your debts into one loan, at an interest rate lower than your debts currently hold.

If these options won't help, seek the help of a trustee in bankruptcy. If your debts (not including your home mortgage) are less than $75,000, they may suggest a consumer proposal, which is a formal request under the *Bankruptcy and Insolvency Act* for your creditors to reduce your debts, allow you more time to pay them, or both. You keep your assets, and your credit record reflects the proposal for only three years after you complete it, compared to the six to seven years that a bankruptcy stays on your record.

If you must declare bankruptcy, you will have to declare the cars. If you have equity in them (if you owe less on your vehicle loans than the vehicles are worth) you can keep them by paying the trustee the equity and continuing to pay off the loan. If you have no equity (you owe more on them than they're worth), it makes more sense to give them up and make other arrangements.

Regardless of the outcome, do seek help to ensure that you never have to face this situation again.

10. SMALL CLAIMS COURT

Q: I'm not satisfied with work that was done recently on my house. I don't want to pay the full bill, but the contractor wants the amount we agreed on. Since we can't find a compromise, my neighbour suggested I take the issue to small claims court. What's involved? Will I need a lawyer?

A: Small claims court in Ontario hears civil matters with a value up to $10,000, so if the amount you don't want to pay is $10,000 or less (or if you're willing to accept a maximum of $10,000), it could be your answer. The limits vary from province to province, so check with your provincial small claims court for the monetary limit in your province. It hears three main types of claims: for money owed, for damages where someone has caused a monetary loss, and for the return of personal property. Because it's simpler and more informal than the regular court system, you don't need a lawyer, although you can choose to be represented by counsel.

You must file your claim in person and pay the required fee at the small claims court in the region where the problem occurred. As the plaintiff, you must then arrange service of the claim on the contractor (the defendant).

If the contractor doesn't file a defense within a specified time, you can obtain a default judgment based on your claim. If the claim is defended, a pretrial conference can be requested to bring the parties together to discuss the issues under the supervision of a court officer. Both parties can also offer a settlement to the other. This often leads to solutions.

If you go to trial, you can enter documents as evidence, call witnesses, and cross-examine the defendant and his or her witnesses. If the judge agrees with you, the decision might include a reduction of the bill and an award for your costs (such as the fee to file a claim). Once the decision is entered as a judgment, both parties must abide by it unless it's appealed. Enforcement options are available to you if, for example, you are owed money.

Small claims court staff can help at every stage, and there are detailed guides available, as well. To begin, in Ontario, request the booklet *How to Make Small Claims Court Work For You*.

11. STUDENT CREDIT CARDS

Q: My daughter is only 19 and she has left for university away from home. She told me that during the first week of orientation, she received a brochure for her to apply for credit cards so that she could "establish her credit." My daughter has never had credit cards before and now she has five.

What can I do to make sure she doesn't get in over her head, ruining her credit rating and her life?

A: Unfortunately, she may be your daughter, but you cannot control her spending.

What you can do is ask her how she plans to make the payments on her credit cards, especially if she is not working. Will she be able to pay the cards off in full every month?

Let your daughter know that the interest charges on credit cards range between 14 per cent and 28 per cent, much higher than for a personal loan. After a while the interest charges really add up.

Also reassure her that while university is an opportunity to establish her credit history, it is not the only time that she will have to do this. She will have plenty of time later on in her working life to establish and maintain a good credit history.

If your daughter agrees that she really does not need all the credit cards or that she can't afford to make the payments on the cards, suggest that she cut up the cards or return them to the credit card companies by registered mail and ask that the cards be cancelled, with a written acknowledgment from the companies. In that way, she will not be tempted to use the cards at a later date.

Credit cards are a money management tool. In the right hands and with financial responsibility, they promote good spending habits. Used to excess or inappropriately, however, credit cards can be the springboard to financial difficulties.

Hopefully, your daughter will realize that while credit cards can be a status symbol, they also carry with them a heavy responsibility to comply with the terms of repayment.

12. BUY NOW, PAY LATER

Q: We're looking at buying a new washer and dryer and are tempted to go the route of "buy now, pay later." What's the catch?

A: The catch is that you do have to pay later. If you can't afford the purchase now, you might not be able to afford it then, either. As appealing as this deal sounds, you need to take a very honest look at your financial situation—and the fine print—before signing.

What are the consequences if you can't pay in full when the money is due? Interest often becomes due for the entire time you've had the appliances. Check out the interest rates and possible penalties.

Is there a service charge involved? Most of these deals require a processing fee plus GST and PST at the time of purchase.

Does the deal allow you to make payments against the purchase without penalty before the full amount comes due? This can help you reduce your debt before the due date.

If the interest-free deal has a payment schedule option, where you would make monthly payments, consider that option seriously. You get the appliances now, you don't have a huge bill to pay immediately, and by the time the deferred payment is due you'll have paid off the whole debt.

If you do have the money now, and still want to take advantage of the deal, consider putting the funds into a locked-in, interest-bearing account (such as a GIC or term deposit) timed for release just before the due date.

Another consideration is that some companies allow discounts for paying cash, sometimes up to the GST and PST combined (15 per cent). This can amount to hefty savings, perhaps even more than your funds would earn in one of those savings accounts.

13. BILL COLLECTORS

Q: We are afraid to let our kids answer the telephone because bill collectors keep hounding us for payment. What can we do?

A: The stress of the situation can be very debilitating. We recommend that you do the following:

1. Find all your bills.

2. Figure out how much money your family owes in total.

3. Figure out how much the monthly payments are.

4. Prepare a budget of how much money you spend per month.

5. Determine how much your family take-home pay is per month.

6. Figure out how much you have left over to pay the outstanding bills.

7. If you cannot afford to keep paying the bills at the current rate, you have several options that will ease your situation—and the telephone calls:

(a) Call each creditor and advise them of your problem. Be prepared to give them details of your problem and copies of your statements to prove what you are saying. At that time, hopefully some type of arrangement can be worked out.

(b) If a creditor will not enter into an arrangement, see if you can arrange for a consolidation loan from a financial institution. Ensure that the interest rate is lower than what you are presently being charged and that the monthly payments are affordable over the long term.

(c) Speak to a credit counselling agency. A list is in Appendix "C" of this book. They have credit counsellors who can help you prepare a budget and enter into payment arrangements with your creditors.

(d) You may wish to file a proposal under the *Bankruptcy and Insolvency Act*. By doing this, you make a proposal to extend the time that you have to pay off your debts, reduce the amount of your debts, or some combination of both. To do this you must see a Trustee in Bankruptcy. They are listed in the yellow pages under Bankruptcy Trustees.

8. If these solutions do not solve your debt problems, you can consider filing for bankruptcy. Bankruptcy is a legal proceeding whereby you assign all of your assets, except those exempt by law, to the Trustee in Bankruptcy. This will relieve you of most of your debts. This will also stop legal proceedings against you by creditors, including the telephone calls by the collection agents.

Whichever of these options you choose, it is important that you stop buying on credit. Continuing to buy on credit will only worsen an already serious problem.

14. WAGE GARNISHMENT

Q: We are a family of four. Both my wife and I work, but on a total income of $40,000, we are just getting by. My wife has just told me that her wages have been garnisheed and that this will reduce her take-home pay by 20 per cent. We will never be able to survive. Help! What can we do?

A: Garnishment of wages is a sign that there are problems with a family's financial planning and budgeting.

The band-aid solution is to find extra money to cover the 20 per cent that is being taken by the garnishment. However, to be true to your family and yourself, you really have to find out why your wife's wages are being garnisheed.

In order to obtain a garnishment, a creditor must first obtain a judgment against the debtor, in this case, your wife. This means that the debtor must be sued in court and served with the papers either personally or by an alternate means.

Once the creditor obtains a judgment, they can garnish for a percentage of the person's net wages. The percentages vary from province to province. These monies are deducted by the employer and paid to the local Enforcement Office, which holds the monies for 30 days. The monies are then paid out on a pro rata basis to the creditors who have registered with the Enforcement Office. Check with this office for a list of the creditors.

Once you have determined who is garnishing your wife's money, you can approach them to see if an appropriate voluntary arrangement can be made for payment. If no headway is made, then an application can be made to Court to reduce the amount being garnished. You will have to provide written evidence and valid reasons to support your application.

In addition, your family should carefully analyze its spending habits to see how it is spending money and where that spending could be cut back or eliminated.

If you cannot budget properly on your own, you may need professional help. Consider consulting a credit counselling agency or a Trustee in Bankruptcy; they are listed in the yellow pages under Bankruptcy.

With proper financial planning, your family will be able to deal with these financial difficulties. Good luck!

Bibliography

BOOKS

Abrams, Don. *The Time Buyer: How to Get Time off Your Job Without Loss of Income* (Dencan Publishers, 1986).

Bamber, Lori. *The Complete Idiot's Guide to Personal Finance for Canadians* (Prentice Hall, 2000).

Baughman, Richard. *The Friendly Banker* (Insomniac Press, 1999).

Biehn, Janice, Steven D. Strauss, and Azriela Jaffe. *The Complete Idiot's Guide to Beating Debt for Canadians* (Prentice Hall, Canada, 2002).

Chilton, David. *The Wealthy Barber* (Prima Publishing, 1995).

Deloitte & Touche Inc. *Debt Crisis? Solutions to Your Personal Financial Difficulties*.

Douglas, Ann. *Family Finance* (Prentice Hall Canada, 1999).

Eyre, Linda, and Richard Eyre. *3 Steps to a Strong Family* (Simon & Schuster, 1994).

Godfrey, Neale S., and Caroline Edwards. *Money Doesn't Grow on Trees* (Simon & Schuster, 1994).

Jules, Jill, and Ruthan Rosenberg. Surviving *Your Partner's Job Loss* (National Press Books, 1993).

Kershman, Stanley J. *Credit Solutions: Kershman on Advising Secured and Unsecured Creditors* (Carswell Thomson Legal Publishers, 2001).

Kiyosaki, Robert T., and Sharon L. Lechter. *Rich Dad, Poor Dad* (Warner Books, 1997).

MacKenzie, Warren, and Graham Byron. *The C.A.R.P. Financial Planning Guide*. 1996 Ed. (Stoddart Books, 1996).

Martin, Tony. *Me and My Money* (Macmillan Canada, 1998).

Orman, Suze. *The Road to Wealth: A Comprehensive Guide to Your Money* (Riverhead Books, 2001).

Pahl, Greg. *The Unofficial Guide to Beating Debt* (John Wiley & Sons, 2000).

Pearl, Jayne A.. *Kids and Money: Giving Them the Savvy to Succeed Financially* (Bloomberg Press, 1999).

Roseman, Ellen. *Ellen Roseman's Money Guide for Modern Families* (Doubleday Canada Limited, 1995).

Sander, Jennifer Basye, Anne Boutin, Jim Brown, and Janice Biehn. *The Complete Idiot's Guide to Investing for Women in Canada* (Alpha Books, Prentice Hall Canada Inc., 1999).

The Canadian Securities Institute. *What Every Canadian Should Know About Family Finance* (Key Interactive Inc., 1999).

The Investor's Group Service. *Starting Out: Smart Strategies for Your 20s and 30s* (Stoddart Books, 1998).

Tyers, Paul, and G. Pierce Newman. *Fiscal Fitness: A Guide to Personal Finances for All Stages of Life* (Prentice Hall Canada, 1999).

Waschler, Larry, and Bruce McDougall. *The Complete Idiot's Guide to Getting Rich in Canada* (Alpha Books/Prentice Hall Canada Copublication, 1998).

USEFUL WEB SITES

https://srv260.hrdc-drhc.gc.ca
Human Resources Development Canada
Canadian Retirement Income Calculator

www.alcoholics-anonymous.org
Alcoholics Anonymous

www.attorneygeneral.jus.gov.on.ca
Ministry of the Attorney General for the Province of Ontario
Small Claims Court practice and procedure

www.bankofamerica.com/teenvisa
Bank of America
prepaid credit cards

www.canlearn.ca
CanLearn Interactive
online calculator for secondary education costs

www.cbs.gov.on.ca
Ministry of Consumer and Business Services
a variety of consumer information

www.cbs.gov.on.ca/mcbs/english/2452_3fe.htm
Ministry of Consumer and Business Services
to file a complaint online against a business or collection agency

www.ccra-adrc.gc.ca
Canada Customs and Revenue Agency
tax information

www.clhia.ca
Canadian Life and Health Insurance Association Inc.
various aspects of insurance

www.debtorsanonymous.org
Debtors Anonymous

www.equifax.ca
Equifax Canada
online credit history report

www.gamblersanonymous.org
Gamblers Anonymous

www.hometrust.ca
Home Trust Company
secured credit cards

www.ibc.ca
Insurance Bureau of Canada
various aspects of insurance

www.insurance-canada.ca
Insurance-Canada.ca
various insurance matters

www.narcoticsanonymous.org
Narcotics Anonymous

www.pbskids.org
PBS Kids
kids and money

www.taxwiz.ca
Taxwiz
tax return filing software

www.tuc.ca
TransUnion Canada
online credit history report

www.visabuxx.com
Visa Buxx
prepaid credit cards

www.cibc.com/ca/smartstart
CIBC Web site
dealing with bank accounts for kids

Index

separation, 102-106
setting goals, 10–12
short-term goals, 11
small claims court, 110–111,
    225–226
spending habits 9, 10
stock market, and family home,
    222–223
student credit cards, 226–227
student loans, 87–88
survivor's benefits, 108

taxes
    accountability, 126–127
    and audits, 129–131
    and bankruptcy, 68–69
    and family trusts, 167
    and life insurance, 168
    and RESPs, 122, 164, 165
    and RRSPs, 117, 118–119,
        122–123
    changing filed returns, 127
    credits, 120–121
    deductions, 118–120
    electronic filing (NETFILE),
        127–128
    excluded benefits, 122
    filing returns, 114
    for spouses, 124–125
    for the investor, 122–123
    for the self-employed, 115,
        124

late filing, 116–117
non-filing, 219
Notice of Assessment,
    117–118
penalties and interest,
    115–116
phone filing, 129
planning for, 113
telephone scams (1-900 scams), 96
term insurance, 159
time shares, 96
total annual income, 7, 35
Trans Union of Canada, 44, 45

uncollected debts, 109–111
universal life insurance, 160

vacation, planning, 83–85
vacation scams, 95
variable expenses, 32, 33
variable life insurance, 160–161
vehicle, planning purchase of, 80

wage garnishment, 229–230
wants and needs
    defined, 13
    confusion of, 14, 76
    identifying, 16
    and children, 17
white label ATMs, 91
whole life insurance, 160
wills, 106, 107–109, 153–156, 157
Workers' Compensation, 107

ABOUT THE AUTHOR

Stanley J. Kershman is a lawyer and specialist in bankruptcy and insolvency law as certified by the Law Society of Upper Canada, with the Ottawa, Canada law firm of Perley-Robertson, Hill & McDougall LLP where he heads up their Bankruptcy and Insolvency Department. Raised in a one-bedroom apartment that he shared with his parents and brother, he began working at age eight in his family's drycleaning business, learning very early the responsibilities of money. Stanley credits his humble roots with the financial savvy he has today, and is committed to sharing his more than 25 years of professional experience with those who want to reduce their debts and take control of their finances.